GLOSSARY-INDEX

ABOUT THE AUTHOR

Professor Chou Chin-sheng, born in 1907 in northwestern China, has been associated with the Kuomintang and its educational institutions for most of his professional life. In recent years he has taught Chinese economic history at Kuoli Chengchih Tahsüeh (National Political University) and Chungkuo Wenhua Hsüehyüan (The College of Chinese Culture), both institutions having intimate links to the Kuomintang and the government of the Republic of China on Taiwan. In addition to the work at hand and its abridgment, Professor Chou has written shorter works of current political interest on Tibet and the people's communes (both published in 1959), a one-volume study of Min-sheng-chuyi chingchihsüeh (The Economics of People's Livelihood) (1943), Chungkuo chingchi szuhsiang shih (History of Chinese Economic Thought) in four fascicles (1965, reprinted 1970) and Sun Chung-shan hsiensheng chingchi szuhsiang (Mr. Sun Yat-sen's Economic Thought) in one volume (1968, reprinted 1970), the latter of which received the Ministry of Education's award for studies of Sun's Three Principles of the People.

Professor Edward H. Kaplan, born in 1936 in New York City, received his doctorate in history from the University of Iowa in 1970. His specialty is the Southern Sung. He wrote his dissertation on Yüeh Fei (1103-1141) and he is currently a contributor to the Sung Biographical Dictionary Project under the direction of Herbert Franke. He is the translator and editor of Maxims for the Well-Governed Household, by Chu Yung-ch'un (Occasional Paper No. 1 of the Program in East Asian Studies). Professor Kaplan joined the Department of History of Western Washington State College in 1968 and the Program in East Asian Studies in 1970.

WESTERN WASHINGTON STATE COLLEGE
PROGRAM IN EAST ASIAN STUDIES

Occasional Papers

1. MAXIMS FOR THE WELL-GOVERNED HOUSEHOLD by Chu Yung-ch'un, translated and with a preface by Edward H. Kaplan. 1971. 10 pp. ISBN 0-914584-01-4. Out of print.

2. CHINESE POLICIES TOWARDS MINORITIES: AN ESSAY AND DOCUMENTS by Henry G. Schwarz. 1971. 200 pp. ISBN 0-914584-02-2. Out of print.

3. THE LOVE OF NATURE: HSÜ HSIA-K'O AND HIS EARLY TRAVELS by Li Chi. 1971. 134 pp. ISBN 0-914584-03-0. Out of print.

4. IKKYŪ SŌJUN: A ZEN MONK AND HIS POETRY by Sonja Arntzen. 1973. 171 pp. $4.75. ISBN 0-914584-04-9.

5. TEN GREAT YEARS: STATISTICS OF THE ECONOMIC AND CULTURAL ACHIEVEMENTS OF THE PEOPLE'S REPUBLIC OF CHINA by the State Statistical Bureau, Peking (originally published in 1960). Introduction by Feng-hwa Mah. 1974. xi, 154 pp. $4.00. ISBN 0-914584-05-7.

6. WORKERS AND COMMISSARS: TRADE UNION POLICY IN THE PEOPLE'S REPUBLIC OF CHINA by Merton Don Fletcher, 1974. vi, 148 pp. $4.00. ISBN 0-914584-06-5.

7. AN ECONOMIC HISTORY OF CHINA by Chou Chin-sheng, translated in prêcis and with an introduction by Edward H. Kaplan. 1974. ix, 273 pp. $5.50. ISBN 0-914584-07-3.

8. MONGOLIAN SHORT STORIES edited and with an introductory chapter by Henry G. Schwarz. 1974. xxv, 179 pp. $5.00. ISBN 0-914584-08-1.

9. HAN RIVER CHULMUNTOGI: A STUDY OF EARLY NEOLITHIC KOREA by Sarah M. Nelson. 1975. 176 pp. $5.00. ISBN 0-914584-09-X.

0. A DISCOURSE ON GOVERNMENT: NAKAE CHŌMIN AND HIS SANSUIJIN KEIRIN MONDŌ by Margaret B. Dardess. 1977. 109 pp. $4.00. ISBN 0-914584-10-3.

1. WU TSE-T'IEN AND THE POLITICS OF LEGITIMATION IN T'ANG CHINA by R. W. L. Guisso. In preparation.

2. BIBLIOTHECA MONGOLICA. PART I: WORKS IN ENGLISH, FRENCH, AND GERMAN, compiled by Henry G. Schwarz. In preparation.

Prices are in U.S. currency, prepaid only, and include surface postage. Please make checks payable to: Program in East Asian Studies, Western Washington State College, Bellingham, Washington 98225, USA.

OCCASIONAL PAPER 247

Rebuilding Fiscal Institutions in Postconflict Countries

Sanjeev Gupta, Shamsuddin Tareq,
Benedict Clements, Alex Segura-Ubiergo,
Rina Bhattacharya, and Todd Mattina

INTERNATIONAL MONETARY FUND
Washington DC
2005

Production: IMF Multimedia Services Division

Cataloging-in-Publication Data

Rebuilding fiscal institutions in postconflict countries / Sanjeev Gupta ... [et al.] —
Washington, D.C. : International Monetary Fund, 2005.
p. cm. — (Occasional paper ; 247)

ISBN 1-58906-449-6
Includes bibliographical references.

1. Fiscal policy. 2. International Monetary Fund. 3. Technical assistance. I. Gupta, Sanjeev. II. Occasional paper (International Monetary Fund) ; no. 247
HJ192.5.R43 2005

Price: US$28
(US$25 to full-time faculty members
and students at universities and colleges)

Please send orders to:
International Monetary Fund, Publication Services
700 19th Street, N.W., Washington, D.C. 20431, U.S.A.
Tel.: (202) 623-7430 Telefax: (202) 623-7201
E-mail: publications@imf.org
Internet: http://www.imf.org

recycled paper

Contents

Table

Figures

Box

Preface

The International Monetary Fund's assistance to postconflict countries consists of three main elements: (i) technical assistance to rebuild capacity in key economic institutions; (ii) policy advice; and (iii) financial and technical assistance in mobilizing donor support. The objective is to lay the basis for sustainable growth through institutional development and by addressing macroeconomic imbalances. Typically, IMF assistance to postconflict countries is provided in the context of internationally coordinated efforts with other multilateral agencies and bilateral donors.

This paper was prepared for a seminar of the IMF Executive Board on technical assistance in fiscal and monetary areas provided by the Fund to postconflict countries. It discusses experiences in reestablishing fiscal management in those countries; reviews the challenges in rebuilding fiscal institutions based on experiences in 14 postconflict countries; and identifies key priorities in the fiscal area following the cessation of hostilities.

A number of staff members from the IMF's Fiscal Affairs Department contributed to this paper. Special thanks are due to Steven Symansky for sharing his notes on fiscal institution building in postconflict countries and to Katherine Baer for her contributions to the section on revenue administration. Contributions to the case studies were made by Eivind Tandberg and Giles Montagnat-Rentier (Afghanistan); Katherine Baer, Brian Olden, and Diego Romera (Bosnia and Herzegovina); Nicolas Calcoen and Olivier Benon (Democratic Republic of the Congo); Dominique Bouley and Graham Harrison (Lebanon); Patricio Castro and Helio Tollini (Mozambique); and Graham Holland and Davina Jacobs (Timor-Leste). Helpful comments on earlier drafts were provided by Bernardin Akitoby, Thomas Baunsgaard, Priyaranjan Desai, Robert Gillingham, Eric Lesprit, Thomas Story, Theo Thomas, and James Walsh. Larry Cui and Chris Wu provided valuable research assistance. David Einhorn of the External Relations Department edited the manuscript and coordinated its production and publication. The views expressed in this paper are solely those of the authors and do not necessarily reflect the views or policies of the International Monetary Fund or its Executive Directors.

I Introduction

The proliferation of violent conflicts over the past two decades has taken a heavy toll on life and property. The effects of conflict have often spilled across national boundaries through the disruption of economic activity or the influx of refugees, to cite just two examples. Furthermore, countries in conflict have a high tendency to relapse into subsequent conflicts (Bigombe, Collier, and Sambanis, 2000). As such, the legacy of conflict—and its adverse effects on socioeconomic development—have been difficult for many countries to escape.

One of the most destructive effects of conflicts is the damage they inflict on the social, economic, legal, and political organization of a society—that is, on its "institutions." There are at least five market-supporting institutions: property rights, regulatory, macroeconomic stabilization, social insurance, and conflict management institutions (Rodrik, 2000). Conflicts can damage one or more of these institutions.

Recent empirical evidence shows a strong relationship between these market-supporting institutions and economic growth (North, 1990; Olson, 1993; Rodrik, Subramanian, and Trebbi, 2002; Acemoglu and others, 2003; and Rodrik, 2004). Hence, institutional reconstruction and development is one of the key priorities in the postconflict period. Reestablishing institutions can help to sustain peace by laying the groundwork for a resumption of economic activity. Sustained peace, in turn, can further accelerate the process of recovery in the aftermath of conflict.

This paper focuses on a small but important set of economic institutions, namely, those in the fiscal area. It examines the challenges and experiences in building fiscal institutions and capacity in postconflict countries and territories, beginning with a review of the literature on this topic in this introductory chapter. Chapter II discusses the nature and form of technical assistance to postconflict countries and territories from the International Monetary Fund through its Fiscal Affairs Department, highlighting the importance of donor coordination. Chapter III then provides an overview of the macroeconomic and fiscal consequences of conflict by examining changes in key macroeconomic variables in a subsample of those postconflict countries immediately before the conflict, at the end of the conflict, and for the latest year for which data are available. Chapter IV reviews experiences in reestablishing fiscal management in postconflict countries and analyzes key priorities for rebuilding fiscal institutions in the early postconflict period. Chapter V then presents case studies on the implementation of IMF technical assistance in fiscal areas in six countries: the Islamic Republic of Afghanistan, Bosnia and Herzegovina, the Democratic Republic of the Congo, Lebanon, Mozambique, and Timor-Leste. The final two chapters present lessons drawn from the IMF's involvement in postconflict countries and summarize the paper's conclusions.

Review of the Literature

The literature on postconflict assistance highlights the important role of rebuilding institutions to facilitate the resumption of economic activity and the effective absorption and management of aid inflows. The pattern in many postconflict countries has been for aid to surge immediately after the cessation of hostilities and gradually taper off thereafter. Collier and Hoeffler (2002a) argue that this pattern of aid flows leaves much to be desired, as the capacity of these countries to absorb assistance is rather low in the early postconflict period. This is partly due to weak political and administrative capacity.[1]

A framework for stabilization, recovery, and development should center on three pillars: (i) rebuilding the state and its key institutions; (ii) jumpstarting the economy; and (iii) addressing urgent needs and reconstructing communities (Addison, 2003; and Michailof, Kostner, and Devictor, 2002). An important component of this framework is restoring state capacity for macroeconomic management and fiscal operations. Postconflict countries require assistance in budget formulation, execution, and reporting, as well as in the design and implementation of critical reforms. In the immediate aftermath of the crisis, there is also an urgent need to strengthen the capacity of the state to generate internal resources through taxation to finance

[1]A recent paper by Suhrke, Villanger, and Woodward (2004) challenges these findings.

the reconstruction of the economy and ensure delivery of essential services. Thus, an immediate priority in the early postconflict phase should be rebuilding revenue administration and systems.

Sound policies are also important for success in the postconflict period. For example, sound macroeconomic policies help sustain a recovery of growth and avoid a relapse into conflict. Staines (2004) analyzes the impact of conflict on economic development in 23 conflict-affected countries and concludes that in the post-1990 period, a sound macroeconomic policy stance enabled a faster economic recovery after the conflict.[2]

At the same time, there is a "virtuous circle" between building institutions and implementing good economic policies (Addison, 2003). For example, improvements in public expenditure management and tax administration help establish fiscal discipline. This, in turn, contributes to success in achieving macroeconomic stabilization and growth, thereby providing a more stable and fruitful environment for further institution building.

Strengthening institutions and economic policies reduces the risk of future conflicts. Without appropriate institutions and sound policies, recovery may not be broad-based, high levels of poverty are likely to persist, and the probability of a return to conflict will remain high (Addison, 2003).[3]

Establishing effective institutions and economic policies is also necessary for attracting private investment in postconflict countries. These nations need strong and sustained increases in private investment to support broad-based economic recovery (Addison, 2003). Catalyzing this private investment requires the concomitant strengthening of institutions and the policy environment.

In sum, postconflict peace and economic recovery require improvements in economic policies and institution building in a range of areas. These extend from merely establishing the rule of law to restoring the capacity for policy formulation and implementation. Even within the area of macroeconomic management, the needs for building capacity can be extensive. For example, some countries may need to introduce a new currency or establish new institutions, such as a central bank. The need for building institutions is most pervasive in scope for countries that are newly formed as a result of conflicts. Others may need assistance with budget formulation, execution, and reporting. Still others may require help in strengthening statistical capacity to assist in macroeconomic management. The focus of this paper is on institution building in the fiscal area.

[2]Collier and Hoeffler (2002b) also lend support to this finding.

[3]Collier and Hoeffler (2002b) identify three structural characteristics that increase the risk of conflict, the most powerful of which is dependence on natural resource rents. Their analysis indicates that the risk of conflict is highest when natural resource exports constitute 25 to 30 percent of GDP.

II Postconflict Technical Assistance for Rebuilding Fiscal Institutions

The International Monetary Fund has provided a considerable amount of technical assistance to postconflict countries in recent years. Postconflict assistance as a proportion of total technical assistance provided by the IMF Fiscal Affairs Department increased from about 15 percent in 1995 to about 23 percent in 2004 (Table 2.1). A total of 27 postconflict countries and territories have received IMF assistance through its Fiscal Affairs Department.[1]

Postconflict countries were selected on the basis of having endured a major conflict as defined by the Stockholm International Peace Research Institute. The definition was supplemented by information on the "mag" index from the Armed Conflict and Intervention Project of the Center for Systemic Peace at the University of Maryland.[2] The countries selected met two criteria: (i) the conflicts started after 1970 and were resolved or ongoing over the period from 1990–2003; and (ii) the conflicts scored at least 3 on the "mag" index of social disruption. Conflicts that met both criteria but where state institutions remained relatively unaffected were excluded. In addition, three countries (Albania, Guinea-Bissau, and Yemen) for which the "mag" index was lower than 3, but which were declared eligible for IMF postconflict assistance, were included.

During the past three years, IMF technical assistance to these 27 countries and territories on fiscal issues has averaged about 21 person-years annually. Major recipients in FY2004 included Afghanistan, Cambodia, Democratic Republic of the Congo, Lebanon, Mozambique, and Rwanda. Considerable assistance was also provided to Iraq in FY2004. More than half such technical assistance to these countries was for revenue policy and administration, reflecting the urgent need to mobilize revenue to finance rehabilitation and reconstruction. The bulk of the remaining assistance was in public expenditure management.

IMF technical assistance to postconflict countries on fiscal issues has ranged from providing policy advice to helping countries build technical and institutional capacity through short-term missions, training, and the provision of resident advisors. The IMF provides assistance only at the request of the authorities, which helps promote country "ownership" of the reforms undertaken. Progress in implementing technical assistance recommendations is given significant weight in sustaining the assistance over time.

In general, IMF technical assistance to postconflict countries on fiscal issues has focused on the design of the overall strategy for rebuilding or establishing fiscal institutions. A first step in the process has been to field an assessment mission to evaluate existing fiscal institutions and procedures and identify areas requiring technical assistance. Donors have typically participated in such missions, which has facilitated agreement among the key technical assistance providers on a common strategy of fiscal management. This has been followed up with smaller, more specialized missions by the IMF, other multilateral institutions, and donors directed toward specific areas of assistance. In the initial stages, assistance often has been provided through long-term advisors.

Establishing or rebuilding fiscal institutions also depends on successful implementation of reforms in other areas, especially strengthening a nation's central bank and central statistics office. Particularly in newly formed countries, it is critical to develop an efficient banking system capable of providing nationwide cashier and payment facilities to assist in the effective delivery of government services.

Donor Coordination

As noted above, IMF technical assistance to postconflict countries has been provided in the context of

[1]The 27 countries and territories are the Islamic Republic of Afghanistan, Albania, Algeria, Angola, Bosnia and Herzegovina, Burundi, Cambodia, Democratic Republic of the Congo, Republic of Congo, Croatia, El Salvador, Ethiopia, Guinea-Bissau, Iraq, Kosovo, Lebanon, Liberia, Mozambique, Nicaragua, Rwanda, Serbia and Montenegro, Sierra Leone, Sri Lanka, Tajikistan, Timor-Leste, West Bank and Gaza, and the Republic of Yemen.

[2]Documentation on the "mag index" can be found at http://members.aol.com/cspmgm/warlist.htm. The index measures the magnitude of a societal-systemic impact of a conflict on a scale from zero (lowest) to 10 (highest). Detailed information on the Armed Conflict and Intervention Project can be found at http://www.cidcm.umd.edu/inscr.

Table 2.1. IMF Technical Assistance to Postconflict Countries on Fiscal Issues, FY1995–2004
(In person years)

Area	1995	1996	1997	1998	1999	2000	2001	2002	2003	2004
Public expenditure management	6.1	6.4	7.3	8.7	7.2	8.6	9.7	7.6	7.5	8.9
Revenue policy and administration	8.4	10.6	10.5	12.9	9.6	9.9	15.5	11.1	14.9	12.8
Other	0.0	1.0	1.1	0.0	0.0	1.2	0.8	0.6	0.5	0.3
Total	14.4	18.0	19.0	21.6	16.8	19.7	26.1	19.3	22.9	22.0
(In percent of total IMF fiscal affairs technical assistance)	15.3	18.3	18.2	20.9	15.4	18.5	23.3	19.8	24.3	23.1
Memorandum items:										
Number of countries and territories	15	19	16	16	16	18	21	23	21	24

Source: IMF Fiscal Affairs Department (FAD) database.

Notes: Data cover technical assistance from the IMF's Fiscal Affairs Department to 27 postconflict countries and territories. See footnote 1 in this chapter for the complete list.

overall support provided to these countries by the international community. Postconflict assistance from the IMF is usually smaller and more focused than large-scale interventions by other bilateral and multilateral donor agencies. In some cases, the effectiveness of IMF assistance has depended crucially on complementary support from other donors, such as those that provide long-term advisors and computer equipment. This highlights the need for close coordination among assistance providers.

Coordination of donor technical assistance is a challenge in any country, but particularly in postconflict countries, owing to the large number of providers involved. Proper coordination is needed to avoid duplication of efforts and to ensure the appropriate sequencing of technical assistance. Such coordination also helps avoid placing unnecessary burdens on the weak administrative capacity of postconflict countries and ensures that technical and financial assistance is channeled in accordance with the priorities established by the national authorities.

In some postconflict countries, such as Cambodia, Mozambique, and Yemen, the IMF has taken the lead role in coordinating technical assistance. Whenever the authorities have requested it, comprehensive medium-term action plans for provision of technical assistance have been drawn up based on a series of diagnostic and assessment missions. These plans identify the objectives, types and amount of assistance required, costs and potential funding sources, government commitment and counterparts, management and administrative arrangements, implementation benchmarks and performance indicators, and reporting and evaluation requirements. Such plans provide a framework for prioritizing technical assistance needs and building country ownership and commitment, as well as for mobilizing and coordinating donor support for technical assistance.

III Macroeconomic and Fiscal Setting in Postconflict Countries

The challenges facing postconflict countries can be gauged by the economic conditions confronting them in the aftermath of a conflict.[1] Figures 3.1 to 3.6 present information, to the extent that data are available, on macroeconomic and fiscal conditions in 14 countries and territories with conflict episodes from 1990–2003: the Islamic Republic of Afghanistan, Albania, Bosnia and Herzegovina, Cambodia, Democratic Republic of the Congo, Croatia, Lebanon, Liberia, Mozambique, Rwanda, Serbia and Montenegro, Sierra Leone, Tajikistan, and the Republic of Yemen.[2]

Of course, a host of factors besides the conflict influenced the evolution of the macroeconomic variables over this period, so the analysis in this chapter should be interpreted with caution. In addition, the sample size for some of the macroeconomic and fiscal variables differs. Given those caveats, it can nevertheless be stated that macroeconomic imbalances in the postconflict episodes analyzed here—already severe at the onset of the conflict—were generally exacerbated by the hostilities. On average, real gross domestic product (GDP) fell significantly in these countries during the conflict (Figures 3.1 and 3.2), which is consistent with earlier studies on the economic consequences of conflict.[3] Both real GDP and real per capita GDP were below their preconflict levels when the IMF carried out its first postconflict technical assistance mission.[4] Inflation, already at high levels before the onset of hostilities, increased further during the conflict episode (Figure 3.3).

Figure 3.1. Real GDP Growth in Selected Postconflict Countries
(Annual percent change)

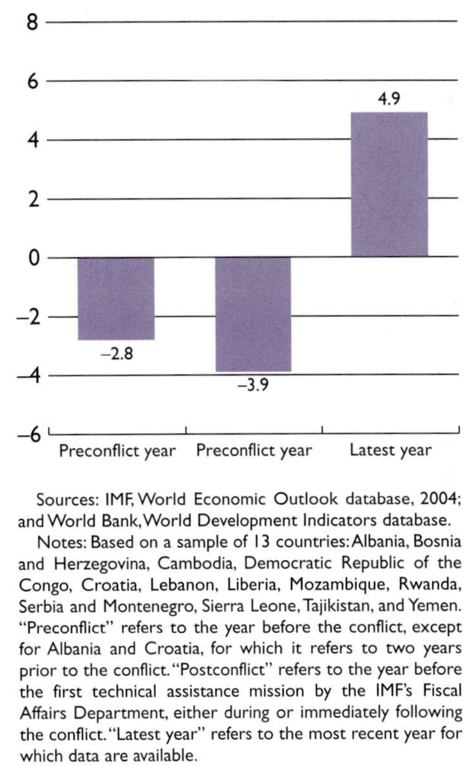

Sources: IMF, World Economic Outlook database, 2004; and World Bank, World Development Indicators database.

Notes: Based on a sample of 13 countries: Albania, Bosnia and Herzegovina, Cambodia, Democratic Republic of the Congo, Croatia, Lebanon, Liberia, Mozambique, Rwanda, Serbia and Montenegro, Sierra Leone, Tajikistan, and Yemen. "Preconflict" refers to the year before the conflict, except for Albania and Croatia, for which it refers to two years prior to the conflict. "Postconflict" refers to the year before the first technical assistance mission by the IMF's Fiscal Affairs Department, either during or immediately following the conflict. "Latest year" refers to the most recent year for which data are available.

Macroeconomic challenges were particularly severe in the fiscal area. The overall fiscal deficit (including grants) increased only slightly during the conflict (Figure 3.4), but underlying fiscal developments were much more adverse than suggested by changes in the deficit.[5] Total rev-

[1]In a more comprehensive study of the relationship between conflict episodes and economic performance, Staines (2004) documents how recent conflicts have become shorter but have resulted in more severe contractions in economic activity, followed by a stronger recovery of growth.

[2]The 14 are a subset of the 27 postconflict countries or territories identified in Chapter II.

[3]See Collier (1999), Collier and others (2003), and Gupta and others (2004).

[4]In the figures, "preconflict" refers to the year before the start of the conflict, and "postconflict" refers to the year before the first postconflict technical assistance mission by the International Monetary Fund. In most cases, the IMF mission coincides with the final year of the conflict, but in four countries—Croatia, Liberia, Sierra Leone, and Tajikistan—the first mission actually took place during the conflict. The "latest year" refers to the most recent year for which data are available.

[5]Excluding grants, the overall fiscal deficit worsened by about 2 percent of GDP.

Figure 3.2. Real GDP and GDP per Capita in Selected Postconflict Countries
(Index, preconflict = 100)

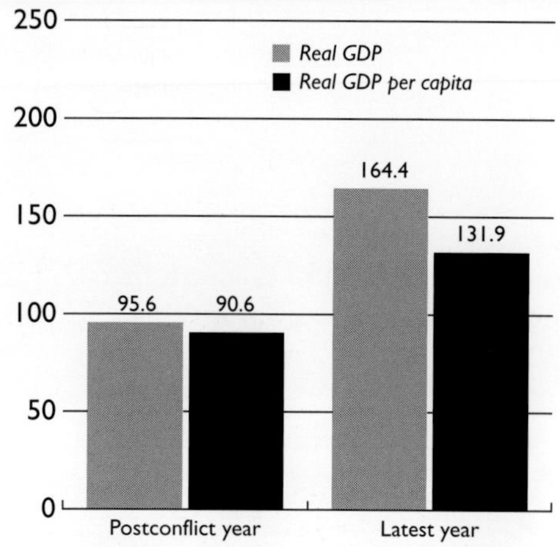

Sources: IMF, World Economic Outlook database, 2004; and World Bank, World Development Indicators database.
Notes: Based on a sample of 13 countries: Albania, Bosnia and Herzegovina, Cambodia, Democratic Republic of the Congo, Croatia, Lebanon, Liberia, Mozambique, Rwanda, Serbia and Montenegro, Sierra Leone, Tajikistan, and Yemen. See notes to Figure 3.1 for definitions of "postconflict" and "latest" years.

Figure 3.4. Fiscal Aggregates in Selected Postconflict Countries
(In percent of GDP)

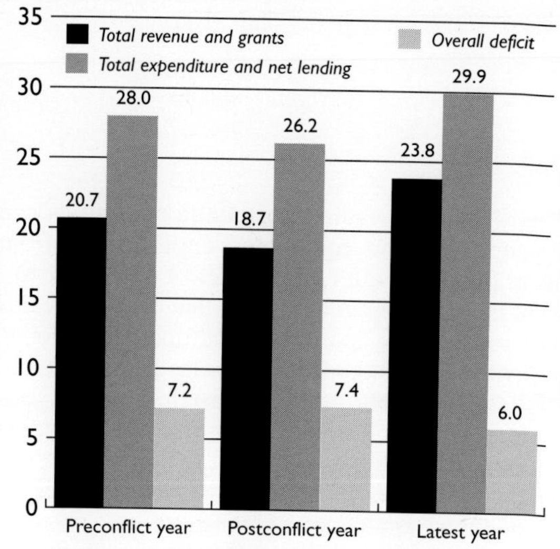

Sources: National authorities and IMF staff estimates.
Notes: Based on a sample of 10 countries: Albania, Cambodia, Democratic Republic of the Congo, Croatia, Lebanon, Mozambique, Rwanda, Sierra Leone, Tajikistan, and Yemen. See notes to Figure 3.1 for definitions of "preconflict," "postconflict" and "latest" years.

Figure 3.3. Consumer Price Inflation in Selected Postconflict Countries
(Annual percent change)

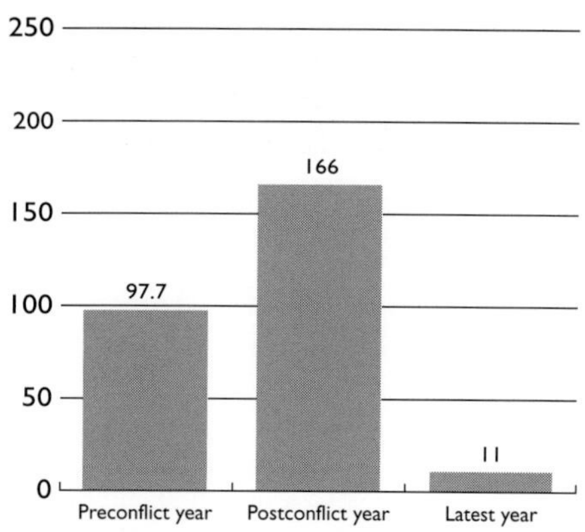

Sources: IMF, World Economic Outlook database, 2004; and World Bank, World Development Indicators database.
Notes: Based on a sample of 11 countries: Afghanistan, Albania, Cambodia, Democratic Republic of the Congo, Croatia, Lebanon, Mozambique, Rwanda, Sierra Leone, Tajikistan, and Yemen. See notes to Figure 3.1 for definitions of "preconflict," "postconflict," and "latest" years.

enues, including grants, fell by 2 percentage points of GDP, reflecting primarily a substantial slippage in revenue effort. In response, government spending was cut back, but not by enough to offset the fall in revenues.[6] Reduction in outlays on wages and salaries were especially sharp, while military spending increased (Figure 3.5). Equally worrisome were developments in the financing of the deficit. Net foreign financing fell sharply during the conflict period (Figure 3.6), forcing countries to rely much more on domestic sources to finance the deficit. Consequently, the domestic financing requirement increased to more than 7 percent of GDP, with adverse consequences for macroeconomic stability, including inflation.

Macroeconomic conditions in these countries have improved significantly in recent years. The latest available data, as shown in the figures, indicates that annual real GDP growth averaged about 5 percent, with all countries in the sample registering positive growth rates. Real GDP was about 64 percent higher than its preconflict level, with real per capita GDP more than 30

[6]In a postconflict setting, there are often a large number of unpaid civil servants and the government is unable to provide even a rudimentary level of public services.

Figure 3.5. Government Spending in Selected Postconflict Countries
(In percent of GDP)

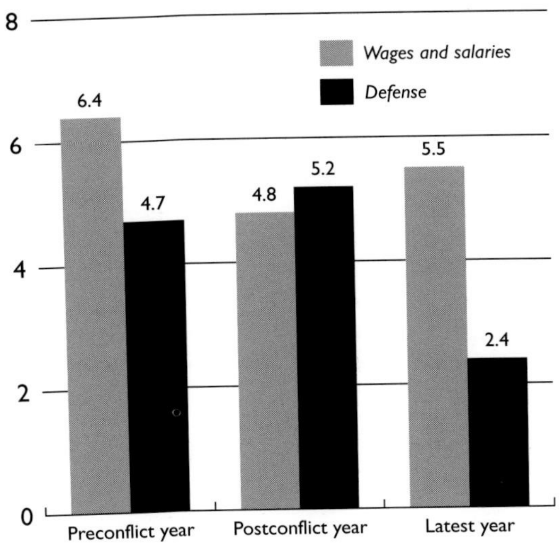

Sources: National authorities and IMF staff estimates.
Notes: Based on a sample of seven countries: Albania, Cambodia, Democratic Republic of the Congo, Mozambique, Rwanda, Sierra Leone, and Yemen. See notes to Figure 3.1 for definitions of "preconflict," "postconflict," and "latest" years. For defense spending, the latest year for Albania, Lebanon, and Mozambique is 2002.

Figure 3.6. Financing of the Budget in Selected Postconflict Countries
(In percent of GDP)

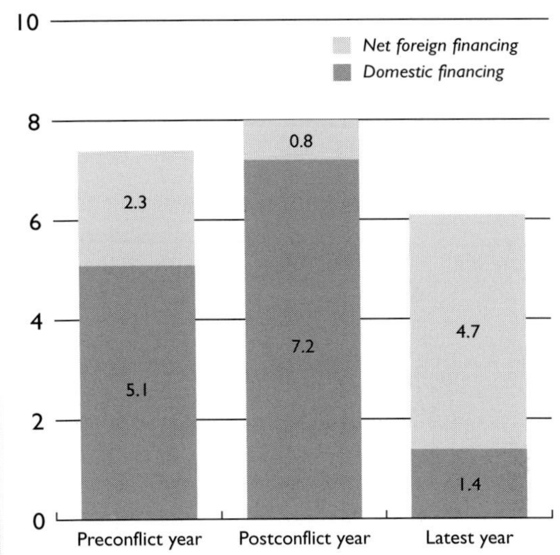

Sources: National authorities and IMF staff estimates.
Notes: Based on a sample of nine countries: Albania, Cambodia, Democratic Republic of the Congo, Lebanon, Mozambique, Rwanda, Sierra Leone, Tajikistan, and Yemen. See notes to Figure 3.1 for definitions of "preconflict," "postconflict," and "latest" years.

percent higher. There has also been a dramatic reduction in inflation.

The fiscal position has also improved somewhat in recent years. Deficits (including grants) have fallen by almost 1½ percent of GDP.[7] More importantly, domestic financing of the deficit has been cut sharply, contributing to greater macroeconomic stability. Revenues rebounded and rose as a share of GDP, surpassing their preconflict levels. Total government spending rose sharply but military spending declined to about half its preconflict level. As such, it appears that the peace dividend has been used by countries both to address fiscal imbalances, as well as to attend to pressing social needs by further increasing government spending.[8]

[7]The overall fiscal deficit excluding grants also fell slightly.

[8]For an examination of the impact of conflict on social indicators, see Gupta and others (2004).

IV Reestablishing Fiscal Management and Institutions

The preferred strategy for rebuilding fiscal institutions in the wake of conflict involves three basic steps: (i) creating a proper legal and regulatory framework for fiscal policy; (ii) establishing a central fiscal authority and a mechanism for coordinating foreign assistance; and (iii) implementing priority changes in revenue and expenditure policies, along with simple arrangements in revenue administration and public expenditure management that effectively leverage scarce human resources.

However, while this strategy formed the basis of the IMF's technical assistance to postconflict countries for rebuilding fiscal institutions, it should be noted that technical assistance recommendations varied across countries due to local circumstances. This caveat is important, especially when country-specific measures are discussed. For example, the sequencing of the steps did not always follow the order above. While establishing a fiscal authority is a necessary early step in countries where no such institution existed before, setting up the authority can take some time. Sometimes, government officials in a postconflict situation may not have the luxury to await creation of a fiscal authority. Certain tax administration procedures may need to be promulgated even if the authority is not fully functional, including procedures for collection and payment of border taxes. On the expenditure side, procedures for government payments for salaries and purchases of goods and services may need to be put in place urgently. In some cases, certain expenditures may be necessary even before a comprehensive budget is prepared. In Timor-Leste, for example, the IMF provided recommendations for executing spending on salaries and purchases of other goods and services until a fiscal authority could become operational.

The relative importance and sequence of each of the steps for rebuilding fiscal institutions also depends on the type of conflict. In general, the three-step framework was followed closely in the wake of conflicts that led to the emergence of new countries or that took place immediately after the creation of a new country Examples are Bosnia and Herzegovina, Croatia, and Timor-Leste.

The framework was also used following conflicts in preexisting countries with widespread institutional damage and social disruption, but the sequencing of the steps was not always the same. Liberia and Cambodia closely followed the three-step framework, but in Rwanda and the Democratic Republic of the Congo, the first priority was to rebuild the basic infrastructure of the ministry of finance, and only later did the emphasis shift to creating a proper legal framework for fiscal policy. In countries where the legal framework for budget preparation and execution was basically sound but had not been applied for many years—as in Afghanistan—other important legal reforms were accorded priority in such areas as income taxes, foreign and domestic private investment, and customs.

Finally, preexisting countries where conflict resulted in relatively little institutional and social disruption did not follow all the steps. In Albania and Serbia and Montenegro, where the conflict was intense but short, fiscal institutions emerged relatively unscathed and the focus of rebuilding was on the third step. In Albania, the immediate priorities included restaffing all tax administration offices, increasing the reporting threshold for the value-added tax, and securing the cooperation of banks in accepting tax payments. In Serbia and Montenegro, the emphasis was on simplifying the tax system to facilitate the transition to a more modern and market-friendly tax environment.

The approach to rebuilding fiscal institutions also was shaped by the role of the international community. In some newly formed countries or territories, the United Nations was responsible for running government operations, which influenced the nature of the advice given. A special challenge in these cases was to ensure that local capacity was in place before responsibility was handed over to national administrators. In Kosovo, a number of complicated legal issues arose as a result of control of the territory by the United Nations Interim Administration Mission in Kosovo (UNMIK). These issues included whether the UNMIK had the right to ignore existing regulations inherited from the former Federal Republic of Yugoslavia and had the mandate to pass new regulations that contradicted these rules; whether Kosovo was accountable for any of Yugoslavia's debt; whether the UNMIK could incur liabilities; and whether the UNMIK had the right to fire redundant workers.

Similarly, in Bosnia and Herzegovina, the Dayton Agreement largely determined the parameters within which the reconstruction of institutions had to take place. For example, the agreements spelled out a highly decentralized fiscal arrangement to accommodate different ethnic and political interests. This led to the emergence of a new state composed of two entities: the Republika Srpska and the Federation of Bosnia and Herzegovina. The agreement further mandated the creation of at least eight local cantons, of which only two had functioning administrations.

The postconflict period sometimes provided an opportunity for bold changes. In some cases, there was openness to new approaches that had been previously rejected as being politically, legally, or administratively infeasible. Thus, while administrative capacity may have been depleted in these cases—examples are Kosovo and Timor-Leste—the immediate postconflict period provided an opportunity to put in place major improvements in policies and institutions relative to the preconflict period.

Creating a Proper Legal and Regulatory Framework for Fiscal Policy

Fiscal operations in any country are generally anchored in two main legal sources: the constitution and tax and budget laws. The constitution usually specifies the division of taxing powers between different levels of government, and between the executive, the legislature, and the judiciary. It also determines the nature of emergency powers available to the executive. Tax laws are critical to make tax policy legally enforceable. They define the powers of the tax administration to collect information about taxpayers and the administrative actions that can be taken against individuals or entities that evade taxes or accumulate tax arrears. New or revised financial regulations are also indispensable to ensure that the fiscal authority is vested with the legal power to control and manage public spending.

The creation of a consolidated package of customs and tax legislation, regulations, and directives often was of immediate importance in postconflict situations. In countries where preconflict legislation was not reasonably sound, a key objective was to simplify tax legislation and procedures for revenue collection in order to make them more transparent and easier to implement and administer. In a number of cases, the complexity of existing legislation made tax laws difficult to implement, especially in light of the limited administrative capacity prevailing in a postconflict environment. For example, in many cases the tax code included a wide variety of duties, tariff rates, and special taxes and surcharges. The mismatch between administrative capacity and the complexity of the existing laws and regulations often led to inevitable efficiency losses, mistakes in tax assessments, and difficulties in tax collection.

A number of countries considered the reform of customs and tax laws to be crucial.[1] In Rwanda, the authorities initiated a comprehensive program to reduce tax exemptions and combat tax evasion, including a review of special conventions in the investment code. The Democratic Republic of the Congo adopted a new and simplified tariff law to reduce the scope for smuggling and fraud, and a new mining and investment code to combat tax evasion. Serbia and Montenegro introduced legislation to radically simplify the real estate property tax.[2] In newly created countries like Bosnia and Herzegovina, substantial resources were devoted to fashioning tax laws nearly from scratch to provide a legal framework for a new, albeit simplified, tax system.

Designing a new budget law and adopting the first postconflict budget—sometimes a transitional one covering three to four months—also were key to initiating budget reforms. Formulating an initial budget after the conflict was one of the most important measures to be implemented. In most of these cases, including Afghanistan, Bosnia and Herzegovina, and Croatia, the existing budget law no longer reflected the current institutional structure. The purpose of the new law was to set out clear and transparent budget classification structures consistent with international standards and practices; provide strict guidelines for budget execution, such as prohibiting unbudgeted expenditures and arrears; establish a consistent framework for internal control and internal and external audits; and provide mechanisms for financing budget deficits.

The new legislation also had to address issues related to off-budget transactions, lack of clear classification of budgetary spending, and the absence of well-established procedures for managing foreign aid. Legal reforms related to public expenditure management issues were also critical. In Croatia, an IMF mission fielded one month following the announcement of the government's stabilization program identified an urgent need for a

[1]In several postconflict countries—including Afghanistan, Albania, Liberia, Mozambique, Rwanda, Tajikistan, and Timor-Leste—the IMF's Legal Department provided substantial assistance in drafting these laws.

[2]This tax had accounted for less than 2 percent of the Republic of Serbia's revenue, and yet the law prescribed burdensome procedures for its administration. Revenue agencies had to annually adjust the taxable value of 1.6 million properties based on information collected from 160 counties on sales of new buildings.

strong legal framework for public expenditure management suited for a market economy.[3]

Reestablishing the authority of the government to collect taxes and preparing an adequate budget law formed an important component of the strategy to reestablish the rule of law. The success or failure of these tax and budget reforms themselves depended heavily on the capacity of the state to reestablish order and develop a system of judicial sanctions to penalize those who evade them (Maravall and Przeworski, 2003). Therefore, ensuring that key legislation was in place authorizing the tax and customs administrations to perform their basic duties was high on the list of priorities. The underlying strategy was to start simple—usually with very basic and short laws consistent with a streamlined tax policy. Over time, these were expanded, allowing for greater local ownership as the details of these laws were fleshed out and capacity improved.

Establishing a Central Fiscal Authority and a Coordination Mechanism for Foreign Assistance

Strengthening the central fiscal authority, or establishing one from scratch in new countries, was, in all postconflict cases, an essential step toward rebuilding fiscal institutions. Newly established countries needed to create a ministry of finance, while existing countries had to strengthen that ministry so it could perform a number of basic tasks essential for macrofiscal management. In a few countries such as Albania, Bosnia and Herzegovina, Serbia and Montenegro, and Tajikistan, this also involved the transformation of existing institutions designed for a planned economy into those that would support a more market-oriented system. Although the precise institutional structure, powers, and responsibilities of newly created institutions varied across countries based on specific circumstances, they shared a number of common objectives. Important objectives were to ensure that fiscal decisions not be taken in an ad hoc manner, establish transparency in fiscal operations, secure a minimum level of revenue collection, and ensure that government spending be consistent with the government's priorities. Establishing a set of procedures to effectively control government spending and establish accountability was important for efficient service delivery and to reassure donors that funds provided for relief and reconstruction were being used as intended. Given the dearth of administrative and technical capacity available within these countries, it was recognized that the institutions had to have a simple structure.

The fiscal authority in postconflict countries was designed to perform three basic functions: (i) develop a fiscal strategy and monitor its impact on the economy; (ii) formulate expenditure policy and execute the budget; and (iii) formulate tax policy and collect revenues.

In newly created countries, the new fiscal authority normally consisted of four main operational departments. First was a *budget department* with the responsibility to coordinate the overall expenditure program and prepare fiscal projections (including for tax revenues) and budget execution reports. This department also had responsibility for assessing the fiscal impact of policy measures.

A *treasury department* was responsible for controlling spending and ensuring that it was properly accounted for. The development of the treasury function was closely related to the establishment of a well-functioning payments system, since the treasury department was also charged with moving collected government revenues into treasury bank accounts, rationalizing government banking arrangements to promote transparent recording of transactions, and designing workable strategies for cash management. As noted earlier, external aid inflows tend to increase in the postconflict phase. Therefore, it is important to set up a mechanism for the proper accounting of domestic and external borrowing and other inflows. Where needed, such a function should be integrated with the treasury department to coordinate and control these flows as well as to ensure proper recording and reporting.

Finally, separate *customs* and *domestic revenue administration departments* were responsible for implementing tax policy and collecting tax revenues. In newly created countries where tax policy options were constrained by administrative capacity, it was decided in most cases to place tax policy and administration under unified management. Thus, these departments also were entrusted with responsibility for tax policy. One issue that often came up in this context was whether customs and domestic tax administration should be merged in order to simplify administration. The modest amount of resources expected from domestic taxes was cited by the authorities, in some cases, as an argument in favor of unifying administration. On the other hand, the procedures for collecting these revenues differed substantially, so the IMF argued in favor of establishing separate customs and domestic tax administration departments, with the former entrusted with the responsibility for collecting trade taxes.

In some countries, it was recommended that a macrofiscal unit be established to help support policy formulation. In Albania, Bosnia and Herzegovina, Croatia,

[3]The existing legal framework required further delineation of revenue and expenditure allocations for the new layers of government envisioned under the authorities' fiscal decentralization plans. Legislative amendments were also required to strengthen the authority of the ministry of finance for fiscal management and provide the basis for a modernized treasury.

Kosovo, and Liberia, the unit was expected to provide advice on general fiscal policy issues and formulation of the budget. More specifically, it was designed to assist the ministry of finance in preparing revenue forecasts for the budget year and fiscal policy scenarios. The unit's tasks included preparing a medium-term expenditure framework, conducting debt sustainability analysis, analyzing tax policy issues, and assessing structural fiscal issues such as pension reform. The timeframe for the establishment of this unit varied depending on country-specific circumstances. For example, establishment of the macrofiscal unit was recommended as a medium-term measure in Rwanda, while in Afghanistan it was seen as a measure of immediate importance, as the new unit was intended to address the limited capacity for economic analysis within the ministry of finance.

Many postconflict countries also needed a mechanism to facilitate coordination of donor funds. In some instances, there were no procedural arrangements for the use of foreign aid, and insufficient coordination between donor agencies and the ministry of finance. In these cases, there was often a disconnect between expenditure needs and budgetary outlays. Better coordination was thus seen as essential for both donors and recipient countries. From the perspective of the donors, information on activities of other donors in specific areas was useful for framing their own assistance strategies and avoiding duplication. For the recipients, such a mechanism provided the spending agencies with information on activities of donors in their area of competence, and thus helped in framing their plans for spending financed from domestic resources. In addition, donor-financed projects also gave rise to future recurrent spending requirements, which needed to be incorporated into future spending plans. In some countries (such as Kosovo and Mozambique), a separate unit was set up as part of the ministry of finance or its equivalent institution to coordinate with donors. In Afghanistan and Timor-Leste, however, a multidonor trust fund was set up to carry out the coordination function. In Timor-Leste, frequent donor meetings also provided an opportunity to better coordinate assistance.

In some cases, establishing and consolidating the power of the central fiscal authority posed challenges for the difficult political equilibria reached during resolution of the conflict. In Bosnia and Herzegovina, Croatia, and the Democratic Republic of the Congo, issues of fiscal federalism/decentralization quickly acquired importance, given the strength of subnational and regional political forces with strong secessionist roots. In these countries, it became important to follow a strategy under which the decentralization necessary to keep the peace following ethnically based conflicts did not endanger economic reforms and fiscal management.

The IMF recommended a flexible approach to fiscal decentralization in postconflict countries to address these concerns. For decentralization to be successful and consistent with sound macrofiscal management, adequate administrative and institutional capacity at the subnational levels is viewed as critical. The IMF thus recommended that fiscal decentralization proceed flexibly over the medium term in tandem with the development of local capacity. In the Democratic Republic of the Congo, it was recommended that the transfer of responsibilities to subnational governments be linked to progress in building local capacity, and that the share of revenues transferred to local governments be determined in the annual budget, rather than explicitly stated in the decentralization law. In Bosnia and Herzegovina, local capacity was either disrupted or nonexistent, even though the postconflict political consensus had devolved significant responsibilities to subnational governments. While the existing distribution of responsibilities among different levels of government was generally seen as appropriate, it was nevertheless recommended that these arrangements be reviewed to take account of changing circumstances.

In countries such as Bosnia and Herzegovina, Croatia, and the Democratic Republic of the Congo, the IMF's advice on decentralization focused on the overall framework governing intergovernmental fiscal affairs as they related to clarifying revenue and expenditure assignments among the different levels of government.[4] The devolution of authority to subnational governments sometimes called for the creation of new institutions to coordinate policies and reduce undesired tax competition (e.g., Bosnia and Herzegovina). Also in Bosnia and Herzegovina, as well as in Croatia, an important issue was the role of intergovernmental fiscal relations in addressing regional income disparities. In such cases, the IMF recommended a transparent revenue-sharing mechanism, a system of equalization grants, and restrictions and clear rules on subnational government borrowing.

Implementing Policy Changes and Administrative Arrangements to Leverage Scarce Human Resources

A number of recommendations focused on actions to reform tax policies, strengthen tax administration, improve expenditure policies, and bolster expenditure

[4]The IMF typically has not provided assistance for institution building at the subnational levels. This task has been undertaken by other multilateral institutions and donors. In the Democratic Republic of the Congo, the World Bank provided advice on strengthening fiscal management capacity at the provincial level. The World Bank also has capacity-building projects aimed at local levels of government in Bosnia and Herzegovina. The U.S. Agency for International Development has provided assistance to Bosnia and Herzegovina for strengthening local public sector accounting.

management and control.[5] In some cases, these actions were to be taken at the time that enabling laws were passed (see earlier discussion).

Policies to Mobilize Revenues

Mobilizing domestic revenues in the postconflict period presented a difficult challenge. The task was complicated in some countries where the tax base was limited in the immediate aftermath of the conflict owing to the collapse of economic activity. Such was the case in Cambodia, Democratic Republic of the Congo, Liberia, Rwanda, and Timor-Leste.

The immediate objective of tax policy in postconflict countries was to raise revenue quickly to finance the most urgent government activities such as paying civil servants and delivering basic public services, and to address large macroeconomic imbalances (Cambodia and Serbia and Montenegro). The longer-term objective was to rehabilitate the tax system in order to mobilize revenues sufficient to cover a significant portion of public expenditures. In general, tax policy proposals were consistent with the objective of establishing a fair, transparent, and efficient tax system. However, the strategy for revenue generation had to take into account the state of existing institutions and the capacity available to implement policies, as well as tax instruments in place at the time the conflict ended. In addition, there often was a trade-off between short-term revenue mobilization needs and economic efficiency objectives. Given the limited options available for generating revenues, governments in such countries as Croatia, Liberia, Serbia and Montenegro, and Tajikistan were advised to implement taxes that were less than desirable from an efficiency point of view, or to move only gradually in restructuring distortionary taxes already in place. A major challenge for some countries was that a large share of the tax base—in particular, incomes of people working for international institutions—was exempt from taxation. Many postconflict countries also experienced a large influx of expatriates in connection with relief and reconstruction work. In general, their incomes as well were exempt from income taxation. The differential treatment of expatriates risked creating a culture of tax exemptions, and in countries such as Liberia made it more difficult to implement a simple tax system where all taxpayers faced a level playing field.

The approach to revenue mobilization in some countries and territories was dictated by the tax system already in place and the administrative and technical capacity available at the time. In West Bank and Gaza, the approach was to rely as much as possible on the existing system to raise revenues in the short run, and delay major policy initiatives until sufficient capacity had been rebuilt. In some countries, major sources of revenues remained largely unaffected by the conflict or were quickly rehabilitated after the cessation of hostilities. In those countries—examples are Albania and Sierra Leone—assistance in the early postconflict period focused on restoring capacity in revenue administration. Tax instruments were left largely intact, except for modifications to make them simpler, more transparent, and easier to implement. Sometimes emphasis was also placed on the collection of arrears, as in Yemen, where a key IMF recommendation was to accelerate collection of tax arrears from public enterprises, as well as arrears on profit transfers to the budget. Where conflict had so severely damaged capacity that the existing system could not be implemented effectively—as was the case in Rwanda, Tajikistan, and West Bank and Gaza—the approach was to simplify and streamline the system by reducing the number of taxes, harmonizing rates, and reducing exemptions. In countries such as Bosnia and Herzegovina, capacity was so depleted after the conflict that only border taxes provided a significant source of revenue, even though the country's existing tax system—on paper—was quite satisfactory.

In most postconflict countries, revenue mobilization relied heavily on indirect taxes. In the initial stages, the emphasis was on international trade taxes (including sales taxes imposed on imports). These were relatively easy to monitor and collect, given that there were only a few border points through which international trade could be conducted. In view of the limited capacity available, the structure of customs tariffs was kept simple, and in some cases consisted of one single rate with limited exemptions.[6] A sales and excise tax on imports was also introduced in some countries, again with a simplified structure. In the initial postconflict period, with limited domestic production, imports accounted for a very high proportion of consumption; as such, a sales tax on imports effectively constituted a domestic consumption tax.

Exchange rate policy also had an impact on revenue collection in postconflict countries that were highly dependent on international trade. For example, in the Democratic Republic of the Congo, immediate unification of the official and parallel market exchange rates had a large positive impact on budgetary revenues, since about 60 percent of total government revenue was

[5] Advice on expenditure priorities in postconflict countries has been provided by other development partners, and thus is not reviewed here. In a number of cases (e.g., Cambodia, Democratic Republic of the Congo, Lebanon, Rwanda, Sierra Leone, Tajikistan, Timor-Leste, and Yemen), the World Bank provided advice on expenditure composition in the context of a public expenditure review.

[6] This represented a radical departure from existing practices for some countries. In Afghanistan, for example, where trade taxes accounted for up to 70 percent of total tax revenue, tariff rates had ranged from 7 to 150 percent and were allocated across 888 tariff headings.

derived from a dollar-denominated tax base. In Lebanon and Rwanda, the customs exchange rate was adjusted toward the market rate, while in Yemen, the authorities adopted a unified exchange rate and aligned the customs exchange rate with the unified rate, with an immediate positive impact on revenues.

Some countries also introduced or maintained a tax on major exports. In cases where one or two products constituted the bulk of the exports whose production was quickly restored following the end of the conflict, an export tax was seen as another area for revenue mobilization in the early postconflict period. From an efficiency standpoint, these taxes leave much to be desired, as they divert resources away from their most productive uses. In addition, by retarding investment in export sectors, these taxes may contribute to future difficulties in the balance of payments. To avoid these distortions, an income tax—including on the incomes of exporters—could be imposed, instead of a tax on exports per se. In some postconflict countries, however, this was not a viable option for raising a large amount of revenue, given the complexity of administering this tax. In this light, in countries such as Liberia, Tajikistan, and Timor-Leste a tax on exports was seen as a necessary evil, albeit one that would, over the longer term, be phased out as other sources of revenue became available.

Taxes on relatively easily taxable services such as restaurants, hotels, and car rentals were recommended in Cambodia, Kosovo, and Timor-Leste. A broader tax on domestically produced goods was considered to be unrealistic in some countries, given the widespread destruction caused by the conflict and limited administrative capacity. At the same time, the large influx of expatriates led to a surge in spending at a small number of hotels and restaurants, providing an easily identifiable tax base that could be exploited in a simple and straightforward manner. The fact that the burden of these taxes would fall on these expatriates also made them politically attractive. In the initial stages, this tax was to be confined to a few large business organizations. As administrative capability developed, the coverage of the tax was to be broadened to cover areas such as professional, legal, and accounting services.

In a few countries, changes in administered prices also provided an important source of revenue. For example, in Yemen, domestic market prices of petroleum products were adjusted significantly in order to generate revenue, rationalize the consumption of energy, and discourage smuggling to neighboring countries. This was followed by the introduction of a comprehensive system for taxing energy (or other natural resources) from domestic sources.[7]

In most countries, some form of income taxation was deemed necessary for two reasons. First, policymakers were concerned that if an income tax of some sort were not introduced from the outset, it would be politically difficult to do so later on. Second, in some countries, the income tax, in some form or another, existed in the preconflict period. Thus, although the tax was complex to administer, there was previous experience to draw upon while revitalizing this source of revenue. In all cases, the form of taxation proposed had to take into account the country's available administrative and technical capacity, as well as the loss of some of the tax base owing to the adverse effects of conflict on economic activity and the stock of private sector capital. It was generally recommended—in Cambodia, Lebanon, and Tajikistan, for example—that tax rates be harmonized and reduced to encourage compliance, and that the tax base be broadened by limiting exemptions.

A flat withholding tax on wages was seen as a particularly attractive form of income taxation in the early postconflict period in such countries as Afghanistan, Albania, Bosnia and Herzegovina, Kosovo, and Timor-Leste. The tax had three advantages. First, its administration was relatively straightforward. Second, given the relatively small private sector, most of the taxpayers were public servants or local employees of international organizations working on relief and reconstruction projects. In addition, in some cases (e.g., Afghanistan), the tax initially applied to relatively high income earners. Thus, the tax did not affect the large majority of the population, thereby reducing resistance to it. And, third, in cases such as Albania, Bosnia and Herzegovina, and Kosovo, there was some sort of a tax on wages before the conflict began, and thus the reintroduction of the tax in the early stages of the postconflict period was deemed appropriate.

Measures were suggested for taxing business income in Bosnia and Herzegovina, Kosovo, Rwanda, and Timor-Leste. In the initial postconflict periods in Kosovo and Timor-Leste, for example, a presumptive tax on income was recommended for small businesses. Tax assessments were based on the type of product sold, square footage of the enterprise, or a rough estimate of turnover. While the expected revenue yield from such a tax was not projected to be significant, it was envisaged that small businesses would quickly become a visibly active part of the economy. As such, there was concern that exempting those firms from taxation would promote a culture of tax noncompliance. A presumptive tax was considered appropriate at this stage, as small businesses were not expected to be able to maintain reliable accounts, and audit capacity in revenue administration was weak. For large unincorporated businesses, a similar tax was proposed. In Yemen, a minimum business profits tax of 1 to 2 percent of the previous year's turnover was proposed, in part because the measure could be implemented without the passing of a new law.

[7]Nontax revenues, such as timber royalties and other fees in the case of Cambodia, can also serve as new sources of revenue in the postconflict period.

In postconflict countries such as Cambodia and Rwanda, it was recommended that corporate income taxes be simplified, while in others such as Afghanistan, a profit tax already existed but yielded paltry revenues on account of excessively generous tax incentives. In this latter case, it was suggested that tax incentives be replaced with a simple and less generous tax credit for investment in fixed assets. In other countries such as Liberia and Rwanda, the recommendation was to replace the progressive corporate tax with a flat income tax on all business income. In Rwanda, it was also suggested that investment incentives be streamlined and made more transparent.

Strengthening Revenue Administration

Newly created countries needed to establish a revenue administration (tax and customs), while existing countries, depending on the degree of disruption caused by the conflict, managed to preserve some revenue administration capacity, although it was less effective than before the conflict.

Establishing or strengthening revenue administration in postconflict countries generally involved a two-stage process. In the first stage, the priority was to get the tax and customs administrations up and running. This meant starting revenue collection and registering and controlling the flow of goods across borders within the 12 months immediately following the end of the conflict. In the second stage—anywhere from 12 to 18 months after the conflict—the emphasis was on helping countries design, and begin implementing, a medium- to long-term strategy for reforming revenue administration. Such strategies were designed to fit country-specific circumstances and were based, to the extent possible, on international best practices.

Reestablishing Basic Tax Administration Infrastructure

Once key legislation was in place, a critical priority was to secure the basic infrastructure such as buildings, office equipment, and materials necessary for a functioning revenue administration. In newly created countries or territories such as Bosnia and Herzegovina, Kosovo, and Timor-Leste, often the most basic requirements for a functioning national revenue administration (telephone lines, vehicles, physically sound buildings) were needed before operations could even begin. International financing was made available in several countries for this purpose. In all cases, the IMF worked closely with the authorities and donors to mobilize resources and define their use. Many countries needed to establish a basic information system to enable the authorities to produce revenue statistics and monitor such key operations as the number of registered taxpayers, tax returns filed, and payments made. In Rwanda, the provision of basic equipment and the reinforcement of mobile surveillance and antismuggling operations were deemed an early priority. Given countries' limited capacity, it was often recommended that the process of modernization begin with a few selected tax offices collecting the bulk of government revenue.

Identifying and Appointing Key Staff

An important step in getting the revenue administration up and running in postconflict countries was to identify and appoint key staff in senior positions. This was a challenging task in places like Albania and Timor-Leste, which either had no preexisting national revenue administration or had a seriously impaired one following the conflict, and as such had no pool of experienced government officials to manage and staff the revenue administration. In Timor-Leste, IMF technical assistance was used to help identify a foreign expert who could serve as a "shadow" commissioner. This senior official took the lead in managing the fledgling revenue administration while working closely with national counterparts to train local staff. The objective was to transfer management responsibilities to local personnel in as short a time as possible.

Registering and Identifying Taxpayers

In newly formed countries such as Timor-Leste, legislation was needed to require individuals or companies engaged in commercial activities to register with the authorities. In Kosovo, where a taxpayer register existed, it was used as the starting point. In some countries, however, conflict resulted in important changes in the nature and structure of activities of these taxpayers, necessitating a rebuilding of the taxpayer register. Measures also needed to be taken to ensure that all potential new taxpayers were registered. Therefore, registration-check audits were recommended, along with an appropriate penalty regime for those who failed to register.

It was also recommended that all registered taxpayers be assigned a unique taxpayer identification number to be used for filing their taxes (e.g., Bosnia and Herzegovina, Kosovo, Liberia, Serbia and Montenegro, Rwanda, and Timor-Leste). This system was expected to effectively identify taxpayers nationwide, assist the revenue administration in cross-checking information on taxpayer compliance, and at a later stage, facilitate computerization of tax administration.

Establishing Basic Filing and Payment Procedures

Several recommendations focused on establishing simple procedures for filing and payment of taxes or simplifying existing procedures. In many cases, simple return filing and payment procedures were set up with which taxpayers could easily comply, and which placed the least administrative burden on the fledgling revenue administrations (e.g., Kosovo and Timor-Leste). Tax return forms were simplified to enable taxpayers to calculate and report their tax liabilities easily and accurately. In some countries, the national language changed as a result of the conflict, and new forms were designed to take this into account. Countries were also advised to undertake public information campaigns to educate taxpayers on procedures to calculate their tax liabilities, complete their tax returns, and pay the taxes owed. Internal procedures were also defined for processing tax returns and payments, and reconciling payment information with that of the banks and the national treasury. A well-functioning payments system is necessary to facilitate tax payments and collection, which in turn highlights the importance of progress in financial sector reform for the rebuilding of fiscal institutions.

Creating a Large Taxpayer Unit

Setting up a large taxpayer unit to focus on taxpayers accounting for a significant majority (usually 60 to 80 percent) of tax revenues was recommended for many postconflict situations, including Albania, Kosovo, Liberia, Serbia and Montenegro, Timor-Leste, and West Bank and Gaza. In the initial phases of the postconflict period, enforcing compliance with basic tax regulations was a major challenge. Scarce administrative capacity could best be used, it was argued, by concentrating on the relatively small number of taxpayers accounting for the lion's share of tax collections. In the latter phases of the postconflict period, focusing audit activity on firms monitored by the large taxpayer unit was seen as more effective in helping raise the level of compliance by these taxpayers (and thus revenue) than more generalized approaches applied to all taxpayers. Moreover, it was also envisaged that setting up a large taxpayer unit would contribute to longer-term development of tax administration by providing a pilot based on best practices with respect to new organizational structures, systems, and procedures (taxpayer registration, filing and payment, audit, enforcement, and taxpayer services). Setting up the large taxpayer unit in a postconflict environment, however, was not an easy task. First, it demanded a qualified pool of tax staff who could effectively audit the large taxpayers. This required a higher degree of preparation and training than was often available in postconflict countries. Second, the disruption of economic activity during the conflict made it difficult to identify large taxpayers and assess the impact of the new legislation affecting them.

Reestablishing Expenditure Management and Control

Upon entering the postconflict period, most countries lacked a well-functioning public expenditure management system. The immediate objectives for improving budget management in postconflict environments included restoring control over the expenditure aggregates (fiscal discipline), ensuring that budgetary spending was consistent with the approved budget, and giving donors fiduciary assurances that their money would be spent in line with their objectives. The last point was particularly important, given that most postconflict countries received a substantial amount of foreign assistance for humanitarian and reconstruction purposes. Thus, the objective of obtaining accurate and meaningful information on government spending dictated that donor funds should flow through the government expenditure system. However, donors would only agree to this if transparent and accountable procedures for executing public spending were in place. These concerns underscored the need for giving urgent attention to improving public expenditure management systems.

Ensuring that the budget was executed—and not just that total expenditures were under control—was also a central challenge in the postconflict period. In some countries, budgets were not being executed, given the inexperience of the government. In part, this was due to poor budget planning, with unrealistic estimates of the capacity to implement capital projects incorporated in the budget. This implied that some critical programs for reconstruction were not being implemented.

Some aspects of the public expenditure management system were accorded greater priority than others in the early postconflict period. Two areas received special attention during this phase: (i) ensuring that the central authority had control over all revenues and expenditures (e.g., Croatia, Democratic Republic of the Congo, Liberia, Serbia and Montenegro, and West Bank and Gaza); and (ii) establishing a simple accounting and reporting framework with an appropriate budget classification (e.g., Albania, Rwanda, Serbia and Montenegro, Timor-Leste, and West Bank and Gaza). In countries where a system was already in place, the approach was to strengthen existing systems. In other countries, the emphasis was on establishing basic public expenditure management systems that were capable of timely and transparent formulation and reporting of expenditures and revenues at a fairly aggregate level.[8] As noted above for Bosnia and Herzegovina and Croatia, however, the nature of the conflict in some instances did not permit the centralization of all revenues and expenditures.

In some cases, training was seen as an urgent need in the short run. In Kosovo, Rwanda, and Timor-Leste, an intensive training course in basic accounting, finan-

[8]In Timor-Leste, for example, it was recommended that a rudimentary budgetary circular be prepared to provide key assumptions on such areas as staffing in order for the spending departments to submit their budget requests.

cial management, and computer operations was critical to getting the public expenditure management system up and running.

Since a significant portion of revenue and spending had not been flowing through the treasury during the conflict period in some countries, government accounts presented only a partial picture of the fiscal situation. With a return to more normal conditions, an attempt was made to reduce fiscal operations conducted through extrabudgetary channels by integrating all government revenues and expenditures into the treasury (e.g., Albania and Democratic Republic of the Congo).[9] Another complicating factor was that in the initial postconflict phase, a large part of both recurrent and capital expenditure was financed by donors. In some cases, donors wanted to maintain control over the outlays they financed. This led to an additional management problem—bifurcation of the budget system into a "local resources" budget and an externally funded capital budget, with the latter being outside the control of the authorities. It was recommended that all donor funds flow through the government's public expenditure management system, and that donors avoid establishing competing or conflicting aid disbursement and management mechanisms.

Improved information on government financial flows was also seen as important for ensuring that all public revenues and spending be captured in a comprehensive fashion. In particular, complete information on government accounts in the banking sector was needed to help ascertain the accuracy of data on fiscal outturns based on accounting data. To improve the quality of financing data and to simplify the process of collecting this information, a treasury single account was recommended in such countries as Albania, Croatia, Democratic Republic of the Congo, Kosovo, Liberia, and Serbia and Montenegro. It was envisaged that all government revenues and expenditures would flow through this account, and that over time it would allow for better cash management by consolidating cash resources in a single account.

In some countries, such an account already existed, but was not comprehensive. In such situations, such as in the Democratic Republic of the Congo, the approach was to gradually integrate revenue and expenditure flows that were outside of the treasury single account. In other cases, such as Afghanistan, where spending agencies held literally hundreds of different accounts in commercial banks, the approach was to gradually consolidate these accounts into the treasury single account.

The recommended route for establishing the second public expenditure management objective—a meaningful accounting framework—varied according to country circumstances. In countries such as Afghanistan, the existing accounting structure was reasonably compatible with acceptable international standards, and thus could be used in the initial phases of the postconflict period. However, this was not the case in other countries such as Albania, Cambodia, Croatia, and the Democratic Republic of the Congo. In newly created countries such as Timor-Leste, no accounting structure even existed. There was thus the need to introduce a simple classification system based on administrative units and core functions (such as health, education, security), a few broad economic items (such as wages and salaries, goods and services, and capital expenditures), and a funds/projects classification to facilitate the tracking of funds from different donors. Such a classification system provided for streamlining and simplifying budget documentation and thereby promoted fiscal transparency. In addition, a unified reporting format also was developed in these countries (an example was Serbia and Montenegro) to facilitate timely and transparent reporting of fiscal operations to both the government and donors.

Following the establishment of a basic public expenditure management system, additional steps were recommended to strengthen budget execution. Improved cash flow planning was seen as essential to improving budget management in Bosnia and Herzegovina, Cambodia, Croatia, Serbia and Montenegro, and West Bank and Gaza. A system to control spending at the commitment stage was also recommended. In some countries, such as Serbia and Montenegro, early implementation of commitment control was recommended to contain growing arrears. In others, such as Albania and Croatia, this was a medium-term priority. In Rwanda and the Democratic Republic of the Congo, where a commitment control system already existed, it was recommended that the system be strengthened. A basic computerized system to process checks, record information, and produce timely fiscal reports was recommended for Afghanistan, while in Timor-Leste, computerization was viewed as feasible only for central offices, with branch offices continuing to use manual procedures.[10] Further improvements in expenditure procedures were also recommended, but for the later phases of the reconstruction process. These involved reinforcing the administrative and technical capacity of the line ministries and implementing more advanced training programs, usually with donor financing. Other priorities included drafting manuals on budget preparation and expenditure authorization procedures, as was done in Rwanda. Over

[9]Lags in fiscal reporting were also a concern, even in the postconflict period. For a period of more than six months in Afghanistan, for example, the treasury did not receive any cash transfers from about half of the provincial tax collection agencies.

[10]In most countries, full computerization of the treasury ledger and payments system was viewed as a medium- rather than a short-term objective.

time, it was envisaged that a clear set of procedures for the monitoring and control of spending would also be developed and disseminated to all relevant government agencies.

The gradual development and strengthening of auditing capacity, together with the establishment of a code of fiscal conduct, was recommended as a way to limit corruption, waste, and misappropriation of public resources. In Rwanda, the IMF recommended a review of the adequacy of financial controls and greater clarity of responsibilities of the auditor general's office. In Serbia and Montenegro, it was proposed that the jurisdiction of the national audit office be extended to all public spending agencies.

V Case Studies

This chapter presents case studies on six countries where the International Monetary Fund, through its Fiscal Affairs Department, has provided technical assistance in postconflict situations: Afghanistan, Bosnia and Herzegovina, the Democratic Republic of Congo, Lebanon, Mozambique, and Timor-Leste. Whereas the previous chapter identified priorities for rebuilding fiscal institutions in a postconflict setting drawing on experiences in a number of countries, this chapter will provide more detailed information regarding the six selected countries. Each case study describes the postconflict environment and context in which the technical assistance was provided, as well as the overall strategy for rebuilding fiscal institutions. The studies examine the successes and failures in implementing technical assistance recommendations for revenue policy and administration and public expenditure management. For Bosnia and Herzegovina and the Democratic Republic of the Congo, the studies also examine the issue of fiscal federalism.[1] As mentioned in the previous chapter, recommendations can vary across countries depending on country-specific circumstances.

Islamic Republic of Afghanistan

The war and internal conflicts that ravaged Afghanistan for more than 20 years led to a massive erosion of the government's capacity to provide public services. Whereas many formal institutions remained in place, a significant proportion of them ceased to function due to lack of funding, qualified staff, and other resources. The legal framework for budget management was basically sound and many budget execution procedures were in line with good practices. However, there was little capacity in revenue administration departments where infrastructure and equipment had degraded significantly and staff lacked the necessary skills. Proliferation of levies and taxes imposed by different government agencies and local authorities resulted in a complex tax system. Central control over provincial fiscal operations was very weak, resulting in the nontransfer of revenues to the central authorities.

In the midst of all of these problems were some well-established laws, such as in the tax and audit areas, that could provide a sound basis for rebuilding fiscal institutions. However, the task still was daunting because, in practice, even those systems were not operational and needed updating and many improvements. Moreover, rebuilding fiscal institutions also required establishing a well-functioning tax payments system.

Through several technical assistance missions, the IMF helped design the overall strategy for rebuilding fiscal institutions. In public expenditure management, the legal framework for budget preparation and execution was basically sound at the end of the conflict, although it had not been applied for many years. Hence, the strategy focused on implementing the existing framework. In the revenue area, however, emphasis was on both policy and administrative reforms. In the early stages, the focus was on reforming customs policy and rebuilding customs administration. The strategy and the associated reform plans were endorsed by the authorities and the donor community. Hands-on implementation of the strategy was undertaken through large technical assistance programs financed by other donors. The IMF has played a monitoring role to evaluate the implementation of reforms and suggest improvements through follow-up missions.

Revenue Policy and Administration

Revenue policy and administrative reforms aimed to simplify the tax system and improve compliance and efficiency. In customs policy, reform measures included reducing the number of tariff bands from 25 to 6 and promoting the use of a harmonized market exchange rate in customs valuation. Duty rates for certain excisable goods that were mostly imported (e.g., gasoline, diesel, cigarettes, and automobiles) were also raised. In domestic tax policy, the top marginal tax rate for individuals was reduced from 60 to 20 percent and the personal exemption was increased. The wage withholding tax was restored, but only for high-income workers. A simplified and generous depreciation schedule was also recommended to provide an incentive for invest-

[1]Fiscal federalism was also important in Croatia, which is not among the case studies in this chapter.

ment. Assistance in drafting tax law amendments was provided by the IMF's Legal Department, in collaboration with officials from the ministries of finance and justice. The authorities prepared five-year programs of direct and indirect tax policy reforms. Critical elements of these plans supported by the IMF's Staff Monitored Program for 2004/05 included elimination of generous tax holidays and exemptions that could seriously erode the tax base.

Key recommendations to improve revenue administration included implementing measures to ensure transfer of provincial revenue to central authorities, establishing a large taxpayer office in Kabul and several model customs offices, and extending improvements in tax and customs administration beyond the large taxpayer and selected customs offices. These measures—some of which are being used as benchmarks under the Staff Monitored Program—have been incorporated in medium-term strategic reform plans for customs and tax administration designed with the assistance of resident advisors financed by donors.

Some progress has been made in modernizing tax and customs administration, in line with IMF recommendations. A taxpayer identification system has been put in place and the enforcement powers of tax officials have been enhanced. In the customs department, progress encompasses implementation of international standards for the classification of goods, gradual recovery of customs functions from other agencies (e.g., valuation of goods), and replacement of multiple customs declaration forms with a single form for all types of imported goods. Staff recruitment and training in priority areas have improved in both the tax and customs administrations.

Public Expenditure Management

The strategy for strengthening the public expenditure management system involved a two-stage process. The first stage aimed at promoting minimum standards of budgetary operations and reporting. Most IMF recommendations in this area were formulated within a coherent strategy with clear prioritization and sequencing. Weaknesses in budget execution were to be addressed by establishing a treasury single account, improving cash management, and modernizing the chart of accounts. Simplified and centralized computerization of the public expenditure management system was recommended in the initial phase, with its gradual extension to the provinces during later stages. IMF recommendations also emphasized the importance of ensuring that donor funds were channeled through the budget and the treasury.

The second stage aimed to strengthen government financial management. A key recommendation was to implement a new budget law to address weaknesses in the public expenditure management system that had come to light following a more detailed analysis. Other recommendations included developing a complete and realistic annual budget, ensuring timely budget execution, and gradually introducing medium-term macroeconomic and budget projections. In consultation with the authorities and other donors, the IMF developed a two-year work program outlining the necessary steps for implementing the recommendations.

There have been substantial broad-based improvements in the public expenditure management system in the last two years. Most of these improvements have taken place at the ministry of finance, while improvements in line ministries have been much slower. A treasury single account has been established, consolidating all government accounts; a computerized management information system has been set up in the ministry of finance and will be gradually rolled out to other parts of the government; donor-funded capital spending is increasingly being channeled through the treasury; and a public financial management law has been prepared and is expected to be approved shortly.

Lessons

Afghanistan's troubled security situation has constrained implementation of the strategy, and the pace of reforms has been slow. For example, it took almost two years from the beginning of the reform process to record improvements in revenue administration. This is partly due to the fact that the central government is facing the daunting tasks of establishing its authority over the national territory, while simultaneously addressing severe security threats.

Inclusion of technical assistance recommendations as conditionality in IMF-supported programs has helped with implementation. Many of the tax policy reforms were implemented as prior actions under the Staff Monitored Program. Establishing the treasury single account was a structural benchmark under the program. The implementation of these measures was closely followed as part of program monitoring.

Flexibility in the overall strategy is important to respond to changing circumstances on the ground. The initial assessment underestimated some of the weaknesses of the public expenditure management system, since the mission could not travel outside the capital on account of the security situation. The overall strategy was adjusted following detailed assessment by subsequent missions.

Progress also was slowed by a lack of effective cooperation across government ministries. In some cases the ministry of finance fully supported and "owned" reforms, but the ministries implementing them (such as the ministries of commerce and justice) were not fully on board. This resulted in slow progress in amending the income tax and customs codes. In part, this can be attributed to the fact that in the initial stages, little effort was made to reach out to these ministries. Public expenditure management reforms (e.g., the treasury single account) could also have progressed more rapidly had line ministries been more involved at an early stage.

Effective donor coordination is critical for success, especially when a large number of donors are involved. Coordination between donor programs is needed to ensure the optimum return from technical assistance. To move this process forward, the IMF recommended the creation of steering committees in the tax and customs administrations, and the appointment of a high-level independent project manager, to coordinate donor efforts under the five-year customs modernization plan. Nevertheless, there were several instances where donor coordination fell short of what was needed, with donors sometimes providing advice on the same topic (e.g., energy taxation) in an uncoordinated fashion.

Bosnia and Herzegovina

The state of Bosnia and Herzegovina was created in December 1995 with the signing of the Dayton Peace Agreement. In the immediate postconflict period, many government structures did not exist, while those that did had suffered significant damage. Moreover, the peace agreement mandated the creation of two entities (the Republika Srpska and the Federation of Bosnia and Herzegovina) and a decentralized government. As a result, the foremost priority was to establish the legal basis for fiscal institutions at all levels of government and make them operational. The formidable task of institution building was further complicated by the fact that war-ravaged institutions that bore the stamp of a planned economy were to be transformed to support the move to a more market-based system.

The IMF played a leading role in developing the overall strategy for rebuilding fiscal institutions. Key fiscal priorities in a range of areas were identified through diagnostic missions. The recommendations of the missions were presented in the form of a technical assistance plan, with clear prioritization between immediate and short-term inputs, and clearly demarcated timelines for implementing them. Also provided were detailed descriptions of technical assistance inputs as well as the terms of reference for resident advisors required by the technical assistance program. It was recognized from the very beginning that program implementation would depend on support from other donors, a substantial amount of which was provided by the UK Department for International Development, the European Union, and the U.S. Agency for International Development.

Fiscal Federalism

Based on the country's consensus to have a highly decentralized state, IMF recommendations provided a roadmap for critical decisions relating to intergovernmental fiscal relations. The peace agreement assigned power to various entities to determine tax policies, resulting in areas of overlapping jurisdictions. In these cases, the IMF advised the different levels of government to make clear decisions about lead players and to devise approaches to resolving differences when they arose. Flexibility was recommended in setting revenue and expenditure assignments in the initial period, while there also was an emphasis on identifying a transparent revenue-sharing agreement for the cantons. In addition, tax policy among different entities needed to be harmonized to the extent possible to avert harmful tax competition that could distort the distribution of productive resources and increase compliance costs for taxpayers. Recommendations also called for intergovernmental transfers to mitigate horizontal and vertical imbalances among regions, and for fiscal rules limiting borrowing by cantons.

Revenue Policy and Administration

To help establish viable revenue collection systems, a strong role was recommended for the central government as a revenue collector in order to exploit economies of scale and provide a harmonized tax environment, especially in the context of the planned implementation of a value-added tax. Initial IMF recommendations focused on managing the transition from the retail sales tax to an eventual value-added tax system consistent with European Union standards. Assistance was provided to establish a single customs body at the state level and an indirect tax authority and associated Governing Board. The IMF also provided technical support for implementing the value-added tax. Recommendations also called for rapid implementation of a taxpayer identification system, along with an action plan to modernize tax administration through computerization. Other suggestions included establishing a common customs administration and creating a tax board in order to harmonize procedures, tax forms, and the tax base and rates, as well as to formulate joint tax policy.

The IMF recommended a federal-level corporate income tax based on the argument that this would prevent evasion, head off harmful tax competition, minimize distortions in resource allocation, and facilitate the negotiation of international tax treaties and horizontal equity for taxpayers in different regions. The personal income tax was to be retained at the local level to reflect regional preferences and income patterns.

Despite the difficult conditions in which the reforms took place, there was progress in reforming the customs administration. Advances included the (i) merger of the existing customs administrations of the Bosniac-majority and Croat-majority areas into a centralized Federation customs administration; (ii) removal of internal borders between the Bosniac-majority and Croat-majority areas; and (iii) adoption of a unified external customs tariff. By late 1999, the customs administrations of the Federation of Bosnia and Herzegovina and the Republika Srpska had completed a comprehensive modernization process with substantial European Union support.

Progress with tax administration reforms was slower, although two main objectives were achieved in the immediate postconflict period. In the Federation of Bosnia and Herzegovina, a tax administration law was prepared and approved, establishing the legal basis for the organization and operations of tax administration, and the existing tax administrations of the Bosniac-majority and Croat-majority areas were formally merged into a centralized Federation tax administration. The Republika Srpska's tax administration, customs administration, and financial police were merged into the ministry of finance, and several measures were implemented to improve the effectiveness of tax administration.

Administrative reforms led to tangible increases in tax revenues. By mid-1996, the budget of the Republika Srpska was about balanced, based partly on improvements in tax collection. At the Federation level, revenue performance from customs and excise tax collections was strong, which enabled the Federation to maintain a significant fiscal surplus during the first half of 1996.

Public Expenditure Management

Recommendations in this area were couched first in terms of immediate needs and then more medium-term capacity-building requirements. Three broad objectives underpinned the recommendations addressing immediate needs. The first was to put in place adequate macroeconomic control mechanisms to stabilize the economy and limit the inflationary impact of large foreign inflows in the context of a crippled productive base. Recommended actions included broadening institutional input in the development of macroeconomic policy at the State level, establishing a cash management unit at the Federation level to ensure that revenues and expenditures were balanced, and creating fiscal rules to prohibit borrowing at the cantonal level, at least in the early years.

The second objective was to enable the new administration to use the substantial expected inflows of foreign assistance for reconstruction and development as quickly and effectively as possible. Recommendations included establishing a ministry for reconstruction and development to manage the linkages between donor funding and the different levels of government, developing an action plan for reconstruction with technical assistance, and designing a viable institutional structure for fiscal management at the cantonal level.

The third objective was to transform war-ravaged institutions from those that were more appropriate for a planned economy to those supporting a modern market economy. Recommendations included developing a framework for the budget process and undertaking immediate improvements in budget preparation and execution techniques.

The medium-term objectives were twofold. The first was to put in place a workable budget system for the Federation. Toward this end, an organic budget law was recommended to provide the legal framework for budgeting. In addition, importance was placed on strengthening the institutional framework for preparing and executing budgets in the context of the reorganized Federation. Concurrently, budget preparation techniques were to be strengthened through such mechanisms as better budget classification and improved analytical capacity in the budget department.

The second medium-term objective was to establish a treasury department to improve budget execution. The treasury would exert control over government payments, account for their use, and manage government cash resources. The approach focused initially on preserving and reformulating those elements of the existing system that were workable, so that a treasury system could become operative as soon as possible. It was envisaged that the existing payments bureaus could serve as an elementary treasury system in the initial period. A treasury single account was recommended for consolidating government cash balances and guiding the execution of the budget through a process of cash planning.

The public expenditure management system improved considerably, slowly at first but then at an accelerating rate. An organic budget law was introduced in 1998, spelling out the role of the treasury. A treasury single account and general treasury ledger were established in 2000, and regulations on budget accounting were introduced later that year. Financial regulations regarding the chart of accounts, financial reporting, and annual accounts were issued in the following year.

Lessons

Effective cooperation among different technical assistance providers is essential to any successful rebuilding exercise. Initially in Bosnia and Herzegovina, the IMF recommended a gradual approach to dismantling the existing treasury system, while other providers advocated what could be described as a "big-bang" approach. However, the donors eventually worked together to take a unified stand on the issue. In the end, the big-bang approach that was adopted was not as disruptive as the IMF had feared, mainly because the different technical assistance providers worked together extensively to ensure the success of the transformation from the old payments system to a modern treasury system.

The implementation as well as the sequencing and prioritization of reforms must take into account the fact that some reforms take more time than others. For example, in the public expenditure management area it is possible to establish an expenditure control system in a much shorter time frame than analysis and policy development capacity. In the case of Bosnia and Herzegovina, an effective budget execution system incorporating a treasury single account was established reasonably quickly, while progress in fiscal policy development and in enhancing budget analysis skills was much slower.

Country ownership determines the pace of implementation of reforms. Progress in tax policy reforms was slower precisely because, in the initial stages, ownership of reforms was weak. In particular, it took some time for the political leadership in the country's two constituent entities to come to an agreement on the distribution of powers regarding tax policy and administration. In a similar vein, implementation of public expenditure management reforms also got off to a slow start, but subsequently the pace picked up.

Democratic Republic of the Congo[2]

The end of the civil war in the Democratic Republic of the Congo (DRC) was marked by a vicious circle of hyperinflation, a depreciating currency, and general impoverishment of the population. The primary factor behind this was the monetization of an uncontrolled budget deficit resulting from the collapse of the expenditure control system and revenue collections. By 2001, the expenditure management system had dramatically deteriorated: a large part of government revenue collection and expenditure was being conducted outside the treasury, and government expenditure was no longer being reported in an orderly fashion. The poor revenue performance resulted from a complex tariff and tax system and a narrow tax base due to numerous exemptions and discretionary measures. Significant weaknesses in the revenue agencies also resulted in poor tax compliance.

The IMF took the lead in designing the overall strategy for rebuilding fiscal institutions in the DRC. The strategy was formulated even while the conflict was still ongoing and only about half of the national territory was under government control. An initial multitopic mission in March 2001 was followed by specialized missions to design reform strategies and identify technical assistance needs. A strong resident technical assistance program was put in place along with regular follow-up missions to assess reforms and provide further guidance. The World Bank also provided substantial support to complement the work of the IMF.

[2]See Clément (2005) for a comprehensive discussion of post-conflict developments in the Democratic Republic of the Congo.

Revenue Policy and Administration

On the revenue side, efforts focused on strengthening revenue administration capacity before introducing policy reforms. The strategy for strengthening revenue administration was implemented in two phases. The first phase included measures to strengthen the customs and tax departments (*Office des Douanes et Accises—OFIDA*—and the *Direction Générale des Impôts—DGI*) and set up a large taxpayer unit for the 500 to 600 largest taxpayers (accounting for about 70 percent of total tax collections).

The objective of the first phase of reforms was to restore the administrative capacity to collect revenue from major revenue sources, before extending the reforms to the entire country and all taxpayers. The DGI headquarters was reorganized only in early 2003, and large taxpayer unit operations began in March of that year. Modern organizational principles and simplified collection procedures (such as self-assessment and payment through banks), supported by new computer systems, were introduced in the large taxpayer unit upon its inception. During the same period, customs administration reform focused on introducing a basic management system to provide statistical information and monitor customs exemptions, and establishing a pilot customs office in Matadi (the DRC's main port of entry) to introduce a new organizational structure and simplified procedures and systems (including the ASYCUDA computer system).

The second reform phase began in 2003 with the aim of expanding new organizational principles, procedures, and systems to the entire revenue administration. Relying on the modern processes developed in the large taxpayer unit and the pilot customs office, the program aims to restructure the network of local tax offices, modernize customs organization and procedures, and progressively expand the DGI and OFIDA modernization efforts to other regions, following the installation of a government with control over the entire country. The DGI is preparing to set up medium-size enterprise centers in Kinshasa, and OFIDA has plans to restructure and computerize new customs offices in the Kinshasa and Lubumbashi areas. Implementation of this second phase of reforms is still in the early stages, as organization and procedures in the model offices have to be strengthened further.

Tax policy reforms were introduced in March 2003 following completion of the first phase of revenue administration reforms. The custom tariff structure was simplified by reducing the number of rates from five to three and by eliminating the surtax applied to specific products. In the area of indirect taxation, the turnover tax was reformed by reducing the applicability of the concessionary rate to only investment goods and agricultural inputs and extending the standard rate to all other products, and by authorizing enterprises to deduct the turnover tax paid on their inputs. At the same time, the standard rate was extended to all products subject to excises, and the petroleum product price structure was simplified.

Public Expenditure Management

A gradual approach was adopted for strengthening the public expenditure management system. The first steps were intended to address the most critical shortcomings in the management capacity of the government's financial operations in an environment where a government priority was to curb the budget deficit to fight hyperinflation. These steps included centralizing all revenue and expenditure in the treasury account at the central bank and restoring the authority of the treasury to control and monitor all payments.

These actions were complemented by the establishment of a medium-term strategy to rehabilitate the public expenditure system, implemented with technical assistance provided through long-term resident experts. This strategy aimed at restoring an orderly budget process and facilitating the reporting of government expenditure, and included the adoption of a comprehensive and realistic budget; implementation of streamlined budget execution procedures; monitoring of a monthly cash flow plan; regular data reconciliation and reporting mechanisms; streamlining of government bank accounts; and implementation of a simple government accounting framework.

Significant progress has been made toward reestablishing proper budget management at the central level. Revenues and expenditures are now centralized in the treasury single account; a new budget classification has been implemented that allows for identification of poverty-reducing spending; budget execution procedures have been streamlined and partially automated; and cash reconciliation and management has improved substantially. Improvements are noticeable in all areas of the public expenditure management system, although more so in budget formulation and reporting than in execution.

Fiscal Decentralization

The IMF also provided advice on the institutional framework for fiscal decentralization. Given the collapse of local administrative and institutional capacity in the DRC, the government was counseled to view decentralization as a gradual process. Furthermore, to help evaluate progress and guide this process, it was suggested that an institutional mechanism be established. Toward this end, the IMF mission recommended creating a commission in the senate and the assembly to deal with decentralization issues. To facilitate coordination among different government ministries and agencies, as well as to set objectives, it was proposed that a working group be created, made up of the ministers of finance, budget, and interior, as well as the provincial governors.

IMF technical assistance also focused on the legal framework for intergovernmental fiscal relations. It was recommended that the assignment of responsibilities be the core of any decentralization law. Any transfer of responsibilities would be firmly linked to progress in reinforcing local administrative and institutional capacity. Given the gradual approach recommended, the IMF suggested that the revenue transfer rate be explicitly stated not in the decentralization law, but rather in the annual budget law. The transfer of revenue would be linked to the transfer of expenditure responsibilities.

Lessons

Diagnostic missions in specialized areas were helpful in designing the overall strategy and identifying technical assistance needs in the Democratic Republic of the Congo. A medium-term strategy with appropriate prioritization and sequencing of actions was drawn up for both revenue and expenditure reforms. In the course of the process, the overall strategy was partially redirected to take into account the actual pace of reforms, emerging priorities (such as the need to track poverty-related expenditures and possible decentralization), and the identification of additional weaknesses. Such adjustments call attention to the need for early and regular follow-up missions in a situation where conditions on the ground are evolving rapidly.

The role of the resident advisors was critical in rebuilding fiscal institutions in the DRC. Given weak initial technical capacity in the ministry of finance and limited involvement of other donors, hands-on assistance provided by the IMF through the posting of a resident advisor was essential to effectively implement technical assistance recommendations. However, progress with reforms stalled once resident advisors left.

Greater priority should have been accorded to budget preparation and accounting. The technical assistance program paid excessive attention to providing hands-on assistance to implementing the budget execution and reporting system, to the detriment of other areas. For example, until 2001, the adoption of the annual budget was not completed until late in the year, if at all. This diminished the role of the budget in allocating and prioritizing government spending. A better balance in technical assistance would have resulted in more assistance to such areas as budget preparation, leading to faster progress in these areas.

Close monitoring within the framework of an IMF-supported program helped in implementing the technical assistance recommendations. Some of the recommendations were included as conditionality in IMF-supported programs. Others, though not representing formal conditionality, were key elements of the authorities' program, and their implementation was monitored as part of the IMF-supported program.

The strength of the authorities' commitment was a key factor in successful implementation of measures. Little progress was made in the period preceding the nomination of the transition government. Technical assistance was effective only when institutional resistance waned and political commitment to reform was reiterated by the transitional government.

Decentralization should proceed in tandem with progress in developing capacity at local levels. In cases where institutional capacity at the subnational levels is weak, a gradual approach to fiscal decentralization may be appropriate. This also highlights the importance of efforts to strengthen local institutions.

Lebanon

Lebanon's 16-year civil war exacted a heavy toll in human and material terms. The nation's public finances deteriorated significantly, owing to the lack of central government authority and the inability to collect revenues. Following the 1989 Taif Accord for National Reconciliation, government authority was gradually restored, and hostilities came to an end in 1990. Toward the end of 1991, with political stability returning, the authorities began the difficult task of postwar reconstruction and development, including rebuilding fiscal institutions. Consistent with the authorities' preference, early efforts focused on rebuilding the tax system. It was only later that the effort was extended to the public expenditure management area.

Revenue Policy and Administration

Rehabilitation of the tax system focused initially on customs and domestic tax policy. The strategy was to raise government revenues quickly by relying as much as possible on the existing tax system. Revenue administration capacity, though diminished due to the conflict, was deemed capable of implementing the existing system. Therefore, initially, technical assistance tended to be in the policy area—it was some time later that the reform effort shifted, in a significant way, to rebuilding revenue administration. Even in revenue policy, the initial emphasis was on reforming existing tax instruments rather than introducing new ones (such as the value-added tax).

Tax and tariff reforms were progressively introduced from 1993 onward. The reform of taxes on income and profits aimed to encourage investment and improve taxpayer compliance by reducing high rates. Tariff reform in 1995 simplified the tariff structure by consolidating charges and duties and lowering rates. To boost revenues, excises were also increased, especially those on tobacco, cigarettes, and petroleum products.

Collectively, these policy initiatives contributed to an increase in the tax-to-GDP ratio from 9.3 percent in 1993 to around 14 percent in 1996.[3] Of equal importance, they laid the foundation for subsequent reforms, including introduction in 2001 of a new customs law that included provisions consistent with the World Trade Organization valuation agreement, and in 2002 of a value-added tax. A further major policy reform—a global income tax to replace the current scheduler taxes—is planned for 2007.

Efforts to rehabilitate revenue administration commenced in 1995. The customs department embarked on a modernization program that was to span the next several years. Under this program, customs procedures were simplified and automated, and a self-assessment approach to the release of goods was introduced at ports of entry. The IMF assisted the authorities in refining these procedures and approaches, particularly in relation to the post-release compliance program.

Computerization of revenue administration was an important element of the rehabilitation program.[4] This was intended to provide the impetus for badly needed administrative reforms, given low levels of tax compliance and generally weak tax administration at the time. However, little advantage was taken of the capabilities offered by the system until the introduction of the value-added tax in 2002. The newly created value-added tax administration successfully utilized the computer system, and reaped the gains of a function-based organizational structure that improved the efficiency of tax administration. The introduction of the value-added tax and associated administrative reforms contributed to a further increase in the tax-to-GDP ratio to 16 percent by 2004. However, income tax revenue yields remain extremely low, suggesting significant tax evasion and inefficient income tax administration. Consequently, the IMF has recommended that a comprehensive modernization program be mounted to cover all areas of revenue administration.

[3]The tax-to-GDP ratio subsequently dropped to an average of about 13 percent over 1997–2001 because of the country's serious economic problems.

[4]The Canadian International Development Agency provided most of the support for this program, including financing for the new computer system called the Standard Integrated Government Tax Administration System.

Public Expenditure Management

Efforts to strengthen public expenditure management in Lebanon began in early 1993. The IMF prepared the overall strategy and a set of specific recommendations for improving budget formulation, execution, and reporting. These included introducing a new budget classification, computerizing budget execution, and revising the budget law. A United Nations Development Program (UNDP) project assisted the authorities with computerization. Financing for this effort was also provided by the World Bank. The IMF provided a long-term advisor who prepared a new budget classification, updated the accounting framework, and advised the UNDP team on computerization.

The implementation of public expenditure management reforms has been mixed. Progress has been made in improving the transparency of budget execution. A new budget classification has been implemented and monthly reports of budget and treasury operations are prepared and published. Weekly reconciliation of fiscal and monetary accounts is being undertaken. However, the budget law has still not been revised. While some improvements have been made to enable the ministry of finance to "manage" the spending process, there is still considerable discretion in this regard, and the budget process remains disjointed.

Lessons

Sequencing reforms in accordance with country priorities makes them more likely to be implemented. The overall strategy in Lebanon focused first on tax policy reforms in accordance with the preference of authorities. This led to greater country ownership of the strategy, which facilitated implementation of the reforms. Where sequencing according to the preferences of authorities is not possible due to the nature of the reforms or conditions on the ground, the rationale for the proposed sequencing should be explained to the authorities to obtain their concurrence and support.

Mozambique

The protracted civil conflict in Mozambique lasted for more than 10 years. Although peace negotiations started as early as 1992, when a provisional cease-fire went into effect, the general peace agreement was successfully concluded only in 1994. Democratic institutions were established in December of that year with the convening of the parliament and the formation of a government by the newly elected president. At that time, revenue administration in Mozambique was extremely weak. Both the tax directorate and customs services were in dire need of reform, particularly the latter, which was unable to enforce payment of duties and taxes or control widespread smuggling.

The overall strategy for rebuilding Mozambique's fiscal institutions, designed by the IMF, involved a phased approach that focused first on the most pressing problems. In the case of tax policy, the first phase consisted of tariff reforms. The second phase addressed issues related to the indirect tax system, while the reform of direct taxes was left for the third phase. In revenue administration, problems related to customs administration were addressed first. Based on available diagnostic studies, action plans were drawn up for both customs and domestic tax administration reforms, and for initial planning to put in place a modern value-added tax. The tax would only be implemented, however, over the medium term. The authorities decided to seek assistance from other donors besides the IMF and the World Bank for implementation of the reforms. Overall coordination in the fiscal area, however, was to remain the responsibility of the IMF.

The IMF was not involved in public expenditure management reforms in the immediate postconflict period because other donors were active in this area. In 2001, an administrative unit—UTRAFE—was created within the ministry of finance to coordinate public expenditure management reform. Later in the year, a public expenditure reform strategy (SISTAFE) was launched with the objective of integrating and standardizing budget, treasury, and accounting information, and improving budget coverage, cash management, and the chart of accounts. The government found it difficult to deal with many different donors providing different recommendations, and in 2001 it asked the IMF to coordinate and lead the process of public expenditure management reforms. A basic framework for the reforms was prepared by the IMF in 2002 following a diagnostic mission and is currently being implemented.

Revenue Policy and Administration

Revenue policy recommendations focused on removing distortions, simplifying the tax system, and eliminating disincentives to private investment. Reform of the tariff structure involved reducing both the rates as well as the number of tariffs. A value-added tax was recommended, along with selected excises, to replace cascading turnover and consumption taxes. More recently, the IMF made recommendations regarding the reform of direct taxes following a comprehensive review of the direct tax system. The IMF's Legal Department has also been assisting the authorities with draft tax legislation, drawing on experts with a background in the Portuguese legal traditions that influence the Mozambican system.

Reforms of revenue administration were designed to complement policy reforms, reduce evasion, and enhance compliance. Measures were recommended for comprehensive reform of customs management, with a view to reducing evasion. A key recommendation was to introduce preshipment inspection and privatization of customs management. A new value-added tax service was to be set up, along with a new computerized support system. Preparations are also under way to set up a central revenue authority.

Significant progress has been achieved in transforming the Mozambican tax system and its administration. The tariff structure was simplified by reducing the number of tariff levels from 24 to eight in the first stage and then to five; the maximum tariff rate was reduced from 105 to 35 percent in 1996 and to 30 percent in 1999. A value-added tax was introduced in the same year, and new personal and corporate income taxes came into effect in 2003. In customs administration, a new and more effective preshipment inspection system was introduced in 1996. A comprehensive private customs management and reform project initiated in 1997 resulted in a noticeable increase in customs revenues. Customs operations were gradually handed back to Mozambican staff during the 2000–02 period.

In domestic tax administration, a new value-added tax service, organized along functional lines and staffed with newly recruited professionals, was created within the tax directorate; new audit procedures were developed and implemented by a small number of newly recruited tax auditors; and new computerized value-added tax support systems were set up in Maputo. Institutional capacity of the revenue administration has improved and taxpayer compliance levels have significantly increased. Both are now more or less at par with regional averages. Implementation was also facilitated by incorporating several reform measures as benchmarks and performance criteria in IMF-supported programs.

Implementation of the strategy resulted in a significant increase in government revenues. Total tax revenue increased from about 9.6 percent of GDP in 1994 to about 14.3 percent in 2003, in spite of the revenue losses stemming from tariff reform and other changes in the tax system that eliminated distortions. The authorities are targeting a tax-to-GDP ratio of 15 percent by 2006.

Public Expenditure Management

Following an IMF diagnostic mission, the basic framework for public expenditure management reforms was prepared in early 2002 in the context of the SISTAFE reform strategy that had been developed the previous year. The reform program was to be implemented over a five-year period, with the objective of strengthening budget formulation, execution, and reporting. Early actions were recommended to develop a new chart of accounts, improve budget execution procedures, and introduce a financial management information system. A treasury single account was recommended to consolidate all government revenues and expenditures. Over the medium term, several important recommendations involved updating budget management practices to improve transparency and efficiency and strengthen budget control. Another key recommendation was to gradually extend budget coverage by incorporating own revenues of government entities and all foreign grants and credits into the budget. The 2005 budget was to include, for the first time, own revenues of some line ministries and expenditures funded by them.

There has been considerable progress in the development of the budget execution and treasury systems. The authorities have taken important steps to consolidate government bank accounts. Progress has been made in developing a financial management system and setting up a treasury single account. To strengthen the management framework for the reform process, a local project manager was appointed in early 2004, with special responsibility for detailed project planning and monitoring of progress, as well as for establishing a coherent risk management framework. In November 2004, the central and branch officers of the ministry of finance began to execute the budget through a basic version of the information management system (e-SISTAFE), in parallel with existing systems. Full rollout of the system is expected in early 2006.

Lessons

The initial implementation schedule for public expenditure management reforms in Mozambique was unrealistically ambitious. The reform process has encountered delays and setbacks, which has led to several revisions to the timetable for reform. The current timetable is still very tight, but clearly more realistic than the initial one. The establishment of UTRAFE was an important step.

Domestic institutional capacity has remained a constraint throughout the period. Identifying and recruiting suitable professionals has proved more difficult than anticipated. Training needs were substantial, and even generous donor contributions could not overcome these constraints, given the limited absorption capacity of the staff. The slow pace of the overall civil service reform effort has also contributed to delays in establishing a satisfactory revenue administration.

Strong government commitment and good coordination among donors have been important factors in determining the pace of reforms. Government commitment to the reform process was strong from the beginning and remained so throughout. Donor support has also been strong since 1995. In this context, UTRAFE has played an effective role in coordinating donor inputs in a meaningful manner. A quality assurance group has also been established to identify specific weaknesses and risks in the organization and implementation of the public expenditure management reform program. While some donors initially resisted coming under the UTRAFE umbrella, there is now universal acceptance (as evidenced by progressive unanimity in assessments by the quality assurance group) that this coordination is critical to ensure the sustained progress of institutional reforms in Mozambique.

IMF resident advisors have played an important advisory role in catalyzing reform. In the absence of sufficient local capacity, several advisors were appointed to help with implementation of the reform program. They have focused on providing advice to improve core financial management functions and systems, but they have not gotten directly involved in broader public administration reforms. This has enabled them to play their role more effectively and has contributed to the progress in rebuilding fiscal institutions.

Incorporation of concrete reforms as benchmarks or performance criteria in IMF-supported programs can facilitate implementation of reforms. In Mozambique, this has helped raise the profile of the reform measures and focus the attention of the authorities on the steps necessary to improve the tax system.

Timor-Leste

Widespread violence in the wake of the August 1999 independence referendum led to extensive damage and destruction of infrastructure, displacement of the population, and loss of life. In late October 1999, the United Nations Transitional Administration in East Timor (UNTAET) was established to administer the territory during its transition to independence. No permanent structure was in place that could effectively prioritize spending according to even basic principles, nor was there any spending accountability in place, beyond standard UN procedures. Therefore, the formidable challenge was to create a working ministry of finance that would be responsible for a consolidated budget for the East Timor Administration. Reestablishing the government's revenue collection capacity was an immediate priority. Toward this end, a coherent tax system needed to be established along with a new revenue administration. Urgent measures were required to establish public expenditure management and treasury operations, virtually from scratch, within a very tight timetable. UNTAET needed to put these institutional capacities in place quickly in order to manage public services and reconstruction effectively.

Reestablishing Fiscal Operations

Making the central fiscal authority operational was the first element of fiscal institution-building in Timor-Leste. It was envisaged that the authority would design the overall fiscal strategy, formulate tax policy, administer revenue collection, and coordinate the public expenditure program, including the control and execution of public spending. The central fiscal authority would consist of four departments: a budget department to formulate the budget; a treasury department to execute the budget; a tax administration department to collect domestic revenue; and a customs department to raise revenue from import taxes. It was also recommended that the revenue administration departments take responsibility for revenue policy formulation in the initial stages. An interim set of procedures to execute expenditures was also implemented, with a view to achieving a minimal degree of transparency and accountability until the authority could become fully operational.

Initially, the central fiscal authority was to be largely staffed by international experts. Prior to independence, most of the staff in fiscal institutions were Indonesians, who left following the 1999 referendum. So there was little local capacity left to staff the new institutions. Therefore, the different departments of the authority were at first headed by expatriate staff financed by donors. The next step was to recruit and train the Timorese to enable them to take over day-to-day authority activities.

Revenue Policy and Administration

Revenue policy recommendations aimed to establish a tax system that was fair and transparent as well as simple to administer. The objective was to generate sufficient revenue to cover one-half of government current spending in the first year and most of the recurrent budget by the end of the third year (Valdivieso and others, 2000). The proposed tax structure included a single rate customs duty, a sales tax on imports, a service tax on hotel and restaurant receipts and housing and vehicle rentals, various excises, a wage withholding tax, and a presumptive income tax on coffee exports. An interim structure of fees, such as on airport departure and car registration, was also proposed. User charges based on cost-recovery principles were recommended for public utilities and for use of airports and ports. Not all the measures that were implemented were successful, however. The presumptive tax on coffee exporters had an unduly depressing effect on the sector in the wake of sharply falling international prices, and revenue from this tax became negligible. In the end, the tax was abolished by the authorities.

The rapidly changing legal environment posed a challenge to securing changes in tax legislation. During the period of UN administration, for example, Indonesian law continued to apply. Thereafter, the adoption of Portuguese as the official language required that close attention be paid to the Portuguese version of the laws. Frequent personnel changes among counterpart officials also complicated the process.

The IMF provided operational support for setting up a new revenue administration. A commissioner was assigned to secure and lead a team of experts engaged by other donors, which included the United Nations, AusAID, and the Canadian International Development Agency. The commissioner also was tasked with developing the administrative framework required to (i) support a domestic tax collection system based on the principle of self-assessment, which involved providing assistance in drafting legislation, designing structures, systems, and procedures, engaging local staff, and conducting training and public education campaigns; (ii) facilitate the collection of revenue from the Timor Sea participants (mainly multinational oil companies); and (iii) oversee day-to-day management of the revenue administration department. Procedures were recommended to identify and register taxpayers and to set up a large taxpayer unit. The IMF also provided assistance in establishing procedures for filing and payment of taxes, enforcing collection, and developing an audit function.

A fully functional tax administration was developed by mid-2003. By the end of the IMF's involvement, an appropriate tax law was in place, a full set of processing systems had been developed, and a nearly complete information technology system was installed. Taxpayers had been registered, tax returns were being filed, and revenues were being collected. The department had recruited sufficient Timorese nationals to manage the system. At the same time, extensive training was being delivered. Auditing and arrears collection operations were under way, and a basic taxpayer service was functioning. The number of Timorese nationals managing the system increased, but significant work is still needed to fully develop local staff capacity.

Public Expenditure Management

A key objective of the public expenditure management recommendations was to establish a treasury system that would meet international standards for efficiency, accountability, and transparency. Institutional structures and procedures had to be developed to manage the revenues and expenditures, as well as assets and liabilities, of the East Timor Administration. A comprehensive and reliable financial management information system was also needed to enhance fiscal reporting and support efficient execution of the budget. With this end in view, the IMF recommended setting up a treasury single account, and the IMF's Fiscal Affairs and Legal Departments also worked closely in assisting with the drafting of the budget law. In addition, a capacity-building plan for the ministry of planning and finance was designed with IMF's help. Assistance in budget preparation was provided through the services of a resident advisor in 2002.

The core expenditure management system in Timor-Leste compares favorably with the systems of other low-income countries. A recent assessment by the World Bank concluded that the system meets 12 of the 15 benchmarks used for assessing the capacity of public expenditure management to track poverty-reducing spending (World Bank, 2004). The assessment noted further, however that improvements were still needed in expenditure classification, identification of poverty-reducing spending, and public expenditure tracking surveys to ensure that funds were being used as intended. The biggest weakness of the system was poor budget execution, with significant and consistent underspending in priority areas.

Lessons

The overall strategy of integrating several revenue administration activities into a single agency was beneficial to Timor-Leste. The near absence of any tax policy, law, or administrative capacity when postconflict institution building began made it possible to integrate into a single agency all activities relating to legislative drafting, process design, and policy development and implementation. By so doing, a working tax administration was established in a remarkably short period of time.

The external environment can affect the success of tax policy measures. The decline in international coffee prices, for example, resulted in the presumptive income tax on coffee having a more adverse effect on the sector than envisaged.

The strong lead role taken by UNTAET in reestablishing the fiscal system facilitated rapid progress during the period prior to independence. The pace of reform slowed afterward, however, reflecting the limited capacity of local staff and the waning availability of suitably qualified international experts (particularly those with the requisite language skills) to assist the ministry of planning and finance.

Donor support was crucial in rebuilding fiscal institutions in Timor-Leste. Several donors were involved from the start and provided experts who were instrumental in designing and administering the basic processes, while also training locally recruited staff. This international support proved to be crucial, as domestic capacity constraints were significantly greater than expected. Coordination of donor technical assistance was problematic, however, in the area of public expenditure management, where systems and traditions in donor countries are different, and personnel provided by them were not always familiar with each other's systems. IMF support for public expenditure management focused on developing the basic treasury system and the budget preparation function. Getting basic treasury operations up and running helped demonstrate to donors (especially the United Nations) that, while rudimentary, a well-functioning public expenditure management system was in place.

VI Lessons

A number of lessons can be drawn from the International Monetary Fund's involvement with rebuilding fiscal institutions in postconflict situations. While these lessons are highlighted by the postconflict case studies presented in the previous chapter, many of them also apply to any country or territory where the capacity to implement macroeconomic policies is impaired due to weak institutions (Box 6.1).

Design of the Strategy

A realistic overall strategy should be designed up front and in consultation with donors. It should include measures to get the government immediately up and running to pay wages and provide basic services, as was recommended in Timor-Leste. The strategy should not underestimate capacity constraints and should avoid setting up an unrealistic timetable for implementing certain reforms. In practice, some reforms have taken longer to implement than expected. Experience in Bosnia and Herzegovina, for example, suggests that a basic expenditure control system can be set up relatively quickly, but that strengthening analysis and policy development capacity takes much longer. The strategy should lay down a road map of actions with appropriate sequencing and priorities, and identify technical assistance needs and providers. This can also facilitate coordination of donor activities.

In cases where there is little or no administrative capacity, long-term advisors can play a critical role in building capacity and transforming skills in the early postconflict stages. As capacity improves, these experts should play a more advisory role. In some cases, such as Timor-Leste, the IMF assisted in identifying expatriate personnel who could take up senior positions in key fiscal institutions and work closely with national counterparts to train local staff. The objective was to transfer management responsibilities to local personnel in the shortest possible amount of time. In other countries, such as Cambodia and the Democratic Republic of the Congo, these advisors assisted country authorities in implementing technical assistance recommendations and also helped train local staff. The tenure of long-term advisors varies from country to country depending on the pace of implementation of reforms and development of local capacity.

The initial steps in the process of rebuilding fiscal institutions in postconflict situations should focus on designing and implementing simple revenue policies and administration, as well as public expenditure management procedures. As local capacity develops, these can be upgraded. With respect to revenues, for example, experience in Kosovo and Timor-Leste showed that it is useful to focus on basic procedures for filing returns and paying taxes that are easy for taxpayers to comply with and for the administrative system to implement. In a similar vein, in light of scarce capacity, it was recommended that large taxpayer units be established in Albania, Liberia, Serbia and Montenegro, Timor-Leste, and West Bank and Gaza. For public expenditure management, simplified expenditure classification systems were introduced in Albania, Croatia, Democratic Republic of the Congo, and Timor-Leste.

In framing policies and procedures, it may sometimes be necessary to deviate from first principles. Postconflict countries often face a tradeoff between short-term revenue mobilization and economic efficiency objectives. In this light, many countries have had to move gradually to address inefficiencies in some taxes. Such was the case in Croatia, Liberia, Serbia and Montenegro, and Tajikistan. Thus, policies that are suboptimal from an efficiency point of view may nevertheless need to be implemented for a period of time. However, these should be presented as temporary and phased out as quickly as possible.

Where possible, short-term measures should be consistent with the longer-term objective of moving to a modern fiscal system. For example, taxes recommended for the early stages of postconflict institution building have helped lay the groundwork for a more efficient tax system that could only be implemented at a later stage. Some countries introduced a withholding tax on wages (e.g., Afghanistan, Albania, Bosnia and Herzegovina, Kosovo, and Timor-Leste) and a presumptive tax on small business (e.g., Kosovo and Timor-Leste). As capacity developed, it was expected that these taxes would be transformed into a more refined system of personal and corporate taxation. For indirect taxation, a similar strategy was employed. In Cambodia, Kosovo, and

Box 6.1. Applicability of the Three-Step Approach to Other Countries

The three-step approach to rebuilding fiscal institutions in the wake of conflict, as outlined in Chapter IV of this paper, has applicability beyond postconflict countries. In particular, this approach could well be useful for low-income countries with weak institutional capacity, countries where institutions have been damaged due to natural disasters, and countries emerging from long periods of international isolation.

The approach would, however, have to be appropriately adjusted to reflect realities on the ground, which in these other scenarios might differ from those in a postconflict environment. In countries with very low levels of institutional capacity, the three-step approach would remain largely valid. In others, the legal framework may be sound, but policies and procedures may need to be improved to remove distortions or to match the capacity available. In such cases, the second and third steps would be more relevant. In all of these cases, the country would need a flexible technical assistance strategy, good coordination with other assistance providers, and strong country ownership.

In general, the IMF's policy advice for rebuilding fiscal institutions in low-income countries is similar to what has been proposed in the postconflict context. Part and parcel of IMF recommendations for low-income countries are to implement a withholding tax on wages and taxes on selected services, improve revenue administration by establishing a large taxpayer unit, introduce taxpayer identification numbers, consolidate government accounts, and improve the classification system for government expenditures. The three-step approach to rebuilding fiscal institutions in postconflict situations features the same recommendations.

In many low-income countries, however, there will be less of a need to rely on policies that are second-best. Often the choice of second-best policies in postconflict countries reflects the need to generate revenues quickly, as well as limited institutional capacity in the aftermath of a conflict. The macroeconomic circumstances of many low-income countries—especially those that have achieved a modicum of macroeconomic stability—are such that many of these second-best policies could be suboptimal, given the distortions they entail. If emergency situations require implementation of such policies (e.g., an export tax or an import surcharge), these should only be temporary and phased out as soon as possible. In low-income countries, there is usually a strong emphasis on strengthening tax administration and the capacity to implement tax policies that avoid the distortions associated with these second-best options. In the area of public expenditure management, systems in low-income countries have many weaknesses, but are often in better shape that in countries immediately emerging from conflict. In postconflict situations, for example, there may be no disaggregated data on expenditures. In low-income countries, technical assistance for public expenditure management has focused on needed improvements in budget formulation, execution, and reporting, including through the introduction of program and functional classification of expenditures.[1]

[1]For a recent review of the public expenditure management systems in countries that qualify for the Heavily Indebted Poor Countries initiative, see http://www.imf.org/external/np/hipc/2002/track/032202.pdf.

Timor-Leste, a tax on selected services in the initial stages was recommended. The hope was that the development of this tax base could set the stage for implementing a full-fledged value-added tax over the longer term. In some situations, however, such as Afghanistan and Timor-Leste, tax policy options were constrained by the limited mandate of transitional administrations.

Decentralization poses a challenge to fiscal management in postconflict countries. It is essential to ensure that the decentralization often needed to keep the peace following ethnically based conflicts does not endanger economic reforms and fiscal management. A flexible approach to decentralization can address these concerns. Revenue and expenditure assignments should be clearly identified, with an appropriate transfer mechanism to mitigate regional income disparities. In the postconflict situations analyzed here, the emphasis was on the need to develop capacity for effective fiscal management at the subnational level. Given the IMF's limited resources for technical assistance, however, other development partners had to be relied upon to provide such assistance to subnational governments.

Implementation

The postconflict reform strategy should be flexible enough to respond to changing circumstances on the ground. The strategy may need to be adjusted in the context of emerging priorities or as new issues and weaknesses come to light. The pace at which reforms can reasonably be implemented may also necessitate a change in the strategy. For example, the slow pace of implementation and the need to track poverty-reduction spending prompted a revision of the overall technical assistance strategy in the Democratic Republic of the Congo. In Afghanistan, the weakness of public expenditure management was initially underestimated, as the security situation did not permit mission travel outside Kabul. Following a more detailed assessment by subsequent missions, the strategy was later adjusted. In Mozambique, the initial implementation plan for public expenditure management reforms was found to be unrealistically ambitious and required subsequent revisions.

A strong commitment by country authorities is an important determinant of the pace of reforms. Progress is rapid where the ownership and commitment of the country authorities is strong. For instance, progress was slow in the Democratic Republic of the Congo in the early postconflict stages until the transitional government reiterated its commitment to structural reforms. Progress on tax reform was also slow initially in Bosnia and Herzegovina, reflecting weak ownership at different levels of government, but progress accelerated when the distribution of powers regarding tax policy and administration was clarified. To secure ownership in the initial stages, the reform plan should be simple enough to allow for input from the authorities as time evolves. Where capacity exists, the sequencing of reforms should reflect the priorities of the authorities. For example, the technical assistance strategy in Lebanon assigned priority to tax policy reforms, consistent with what national authorities wanted. This garnered stronger ownership for the overall reform strategy. Furthermore, it is necessary to reach beyond the ministry of finance to ensure implementation of key measures. In Afghanistan, there would have been more rapid progress in amending the income tax and customs codes had there been earlier and more effective consultation with the ministries of commerce and justice. Public expenditure management reform would also have been more successful in that country had there been better collaboration between the ministry of finance and the line ministries.

There is scope to improve donor collaboration. The multitude of donors, coupled with weak administrative capacity, has in many instances made cooperation and coordination difficult in postconflict situations. In Timor-Leste, assistance in implementing public expenditure management reforms was provided by several donor countries, each of which had its own different expenditure management systems and traditions. Thus, personnel provided by one donor were not always familiar with another donor's system or approach, resulting in coordination problems. In Cambodia, the donor coordination mechanism was weak because it excluded key stakeholders such as tax, customs, and treasury directors. In Afghanistan, donors provided uncoordinated advice on energy taxation.

There are several different ways to strengthen such collaboration, although no single measure can be viewed as a panacea. Creating a separate unit for donor coordination can help, as happened in Kosovo and Mozambique, by providing a vehicle to incorporate the input of various donors in the design and implementation of the strategy and for the sharing of information, with a view to avoiding duplication and disputes. In post-conflict situations where such a unit already existed, such as in Cambodia, the IMF recommended strengthening the coordination function by appointing a full-time national program manager. Designation of a "lead donor" to ensure greater accountability can also improve collaborative efforts. In Cambodia, Mozambique, and Yemen, the IMF took the lead in coordinating donor assistance. Finally, collaboration can be improved by establishing a steering committee to focus on specific areas in need of immediate attention,[1] as was done in Afghanistan and Cambodia.

Appropriate conditionality in IMF-supported programs can facilitate implementation of reforms by raising the profile of these measures and focusing the attention of the authorities on the steps necessary for their implementation. Program conditionality complemented the reform strategy in Afghanistan. The IMF's Staff Monitored Program included a prior action for tax policy reforms and a structural benchmark for implementing a treasury single account. Likewise, some technical assistance recommendations were incorporated as program conditionality in the Democratic Republic of the Congo and Mozambique, facilitating their implementation.

More effort by the international community needs to be directed toward developing local capacity. Weak institutional capacity was a major constraint in rebuilding fiscal institutions in all of the postconflict situations where technical assistance was provided. In the initial postconflict stages in such countries as the Democratic Republic of the Congo, this problem was addressed through long-term resident advisors, although the reforms slowed once those advisors left. Donors have provided generous contributions for training, but developing local capacity has often proven more difficult than anticipated, as in Mozambique. In many countries, slow progress reflected deep-seated problems in the civil service.

Progress in implementing postconflict fiscal reforms also has been slow in countries where the security situation is fragile. In cases such as Afghanistan, central government authority over the country as a whole was not effectively established until well after the end of the conflict. This affected the implementation of technical assistance recommendations. It took over two years in Afghanistan, for example, to record improvements in revenue administration. This reflected weak central control over provincial fiscal operations, resulting in the nontransfer of revenues to the central government. The security situation in the Democratic Republic of the Congo also slowed progress by delaying capacity-building efforts for local fiscal institutions in former rebel-held areas.

[1]See International Monetary Fund (2003) for a discussion of a framework for collaboration among donors, including in cases where capacity is weak.

VII Conclusions

Building fiscal institutions in postconflict countries essentially entails a three-step process: (i) creating a legal and regulatory framework for fiscal management; (ii) establishing or strengthening the fiscal authority; and (iii) designing appropriate revenue and expenditure policies while simultaneously strengthening revenue administration and public expenditure management. The sequencing involved in implementing these steps varies across countries, depending on country-specific circumstances. The ultimate aim, however, is always the same—to make fiscal policy and fiscal management effective and transparent.

Four objectives have guided the International Monetary Fund's advice to postconflict countries on building or reestablishing their fiscal institutions: (i) avoid ad hoc decision making; (ii) promote transparency in fiscal operations; (iii) ensure a minimum level of revenue collection; and (iv) ensure that spending patterns reflect government priorities. A first step usually has been to review existing legislation in order to simplify tax laws and administrative procedures, or pass new legislation if existing laws and procedures are viewed as inadequate. The next step has been to strengthen the central fiscal authority, or set one up if none existed. Such an authority usually consists of four departments: a budget department, a treasury department, and separate departments for tax and customs administrations. In some countries, an explicit mechanism for coordinating donor assistance has also been established.

The IMF's advice in many ways has been similar to what it recommends to countries without conflicts, but with important nuances to reflect the realities of the postconflict environment. For example, the IMF's advice to developing countries often includes recommendations to introduce simple income taxes based on withholding wages, create large taxpayer units, and improve budget classification. But this same advice has been tailored to the circumstances of postconflict countries. For example, with respect to tax policy, there generally has been more acceptance in postconflict situations of employing policies that are not first-best from an efficiency point of view (e.g., export taxes), given the urgent need to generate revenue. In a similar vein, proposals to improve tax administration have focused on basic aspects of these procedures, such as filing and payment of taxes and registration checks. Similarly, on the expenditure side, the focus has been on implementing simplified systems such as budget classifications under very broad categories of outlays that can be refined at a later stage. In some cases, the adoption of the first postconflict budget—sometimes a transitional one—became an urgent priority, unlike in the case of most other countries receiving IMF technical assistance.

The sequencing of reforms was also different in postconflict countries. The timetable for implementing reforms that are part and parcel of an effective system of fiscal management—for example, an adequate medium-term expenditure framework—is also much longer. In general, recommendations have had to focus on a large number of intermediate measures over the short term that could gradually move budgetary practices from a crisis mode—during which budgets are sometimes implemented on a three-month basis—to a more normal state of affairs.

A number of lessons can be drawn from the IMF's involvement in rebuilding fiscal institutions in postconflict situations. From the standpoint of the design of this advice, six major lessons emerge. First, framing an overall technical assistance strategy at the outset is crucial for sequencing and coordinating assistance among the multiple providers that are usually active in postconflict countries. Second, there might not be a substitute for posting long-term advisors in the early postconflict phase in light of weak capacity. Third, the initial strategy should comprise simple steps and procedures. Fourth, in some instances, policies recommended for the initial postconflict period may not be optimal from an efficiency point of view, but may still be the best possible alternatives in light of limited technical and administrative capacity. Fifth, while the need for simplicity and administrative ease in designing short-term laws and procedures is paramount, care has to be taken to ensure that short-term policies are consistent whenever possible with the long-term goal of moving to a modern fiscal system. And finally, issues related to fiscal decentralization can pose a challenge to fiscal management in some cases.

With respect to the implementation of fiscal reforms in postconflict situations, there also are six central lessons.

First, the overall strategy designed at the outset should be flexible enough to respond to changing circumstances on the ground. Second, the level of ownership and commitment of the authorities has an important bearing on the pace of reforms. Third—and this is an area where improvement is particularly needed—effective donor coordination is important for successful implementation of reforms. Fourth, appropriate conditionality in IMF-supported programs can facilitate implementation of reforms. Fifth, the development of local capacity in all cases has taken longer than envisaged and needs to receive greater attention. And finally, the pace of implementation of reforms can be substantially affected by the postconflict security situation.

References

Acemoglu, Daron, Simon Johnson, James Robinson, and Yunyong Thaicharoen, 2003, "Institutional Causes, Macroeconomic Symptoms: Volatility, Crises and Growth," *Journal of Monetary Economics,* Vol. 50, No. 1, pp. 49–123.

Addison, Tony, 2003, "Africa's Recovery from Conflict: Making Peace Work for the Poor," WIDER Policy Brief No. 6 (Helsinki: United Nations World Institute for Development Economics Research).

Bigombe, Betty, Paul Collier, and Nicholas Sambanis, 2000, "Policies for Building Post-Conflict Peace," *Journal of African Economies,* Vol. 9, No. 3, pp. 323–48.

Clément, Jean Paul, ed., 2005, *Postconflict Economies in Sub-Saharan Africa: The Lessons of the Democratic Republic of the Congo* (Washington: International Monetary Fund).

Collier, Paul, 1999, "On the Economic Consequences of Civil War," *Oxford Economic Papers,* Vol. 51, No. 1, pp. 168–83.

———, and Anke Hoeffler, 2002a, "Aid, Policy and Growth in Post-Conflict Societies," Policy Research Working Paper 2902 (Washington: World Bank).

———, 2002b, "Aid, Policy and Peace: Reducing the Risks of Civil Conflict," *Defense and Peace Economics,* Vol. 13, No. 6.

Collier, Paul, Lani Elliott, Havard Hegre, Anke Hoeffler, Marta Reynal-Querol, and Nicholas Sambanis, 2003, *Breaking the Conflict Trap, Civil War and Development Policy* (Washington: World Bank).

Gupta, Sanjeev, Benedict Clements, Rina Bhattacharya, and Shamit Chakravarti, 2004, "Fiscal Consequences of Armed Conflict and Terrorism in Low- and Middle-Income Countries," *European Journal of Political Economy,* Vol. 20, No. 2, pp. 403–21.

International Monetary Fund, 2003, "Bank-Fund Collaboration on Public Expenditure Issues," document prepared by the IMF Fiscal Affairs Department and the World Bank Poverty Reduction and Economic Management Network. Available via the Internet: http://www.imf.org/external/np/fad/pubexpen/2003/021403.htm.

Maravall, José María, and Adam Przeworski, 2003, *Democracy and the Rule of Law* (New York: Cambridge University Press).

Michailof, Serge, Markus Kostner, and Xavier Devictor, 2002, "Post-Conflict Recovery in Africa," Africa Region Working Paper Series, No. 30 (Washington: World Bank).

North, Douglass, 1990, *Institutions, Institutional Change and Economic Performance* (New York: Cambridge University Press).

Olson, Mancur, 1993, "Dictatorship, Democracy and Development," *American Political Science Review,* Vol. 87, No. 3, pp. 567–76.

Rodrik, Dani, 2000, "Institutions for High-Quality Growth: What They Are and How to Acquire Them," NBER Working Paper No. 7540 (Cambridge, Massachusetts: National Bureau of Economic Research).

———, 2004, "Getting Institutions Right" (Cambridge, Massachusetts: Harvard University. Available via the Internet: http://ksghome.harvard.edu/~.drodrik.academic.ksg/ifo-institutions%20article%20_April%202004_.pdf.

———, Arvind Subramanian, and Francesco Trebbi, 2002, "Institutions Rule: The Primacy of Institutions over Integration and Geography in Economic Development," IMF Working Paper 02/189 (Washington: International Monetary Fund).

Staines, Nicolas, 2004, "Economic Performance Over the Conflict Cycle," IMF Working Paper 04/95 (Washington: International Monetary Fund).

Suhrke, Astri, Espen Villanger, and Susan Woodward, 2004, "Economic Aid to Post-Conflict Countries: Correcting the Empirical and Theoretical Foundations of Policy," paper presented at the United Nations World Institute for Development Economics Research Conference, "Making Peace Work," Helsinki, June 4–5.

Valdivieso, Luis, Toshihide Endo, Luis V. Mendonça, Alejandro López Mejía, and Shamsuddin M. Tareq, 2000, *Timor-Leste: Establishing the Foundations of Sound Macroeconomic Management* (Washington: International Monetary Fund).

World Bank, 2004, "The Democratic Republic of Timor-Leste: Public Expenditure Review," Economic Report No. 27886-TP, Poverty Reduction and Economic Management Sector Unit, Asia and Pacific Region (Washington).

Recent Occasional Papers of the International Monetary Fund

247. Rebuilding Fiscal Institutions in Post-Conflict Countries, by Sanjeev Gupta, Shamsuddin Tareq, Benedict Clements, Alex Segura-Ubiergo, Rina Bhattacharya, and Todd Mattina. 2005.
246. Experience with Large Fiscal Adjustments, by George C. Tsibouris, Mark A. Horton, Mark Flanagan, and Wojciech S. Maliszewski. 2005.
245. Budget System Reform in Emerging Economies: The Challenges and the Reform Agenda, by Jack Diamond. 2005.
244. Monetary Policy Implementation at Different Stages of Market Development, by a staff team led by Bernard J. Laurens. 2005.
243. Central America: Global Integration and Regional Cooperation, edited by Markus Rodlauer and Alfred Schipke. 2005.
242. Turkey at the Crossroads: From Crisis Resolution to EU Accession, by a staff team led by Reza Moghadam. 2005.
241. The Design of IMF-Supported Programs, by Atish Ghosh, Charis Christofides, Jun Kim, Laura Papi, Uma Ramakrishnan, Alun Thomas, and Juan Zalduendo. 2005.
240. Debt-Related Vulnerabilities and Financial Crises: An Application of the Balance Sheet Approach to Emerging Market Countries, by Christoph Rosenberg, Ioannis Halikias, Brett House, Christian Keller, Jens Nystedt, Alexander Pitt, and Brad Setser. 2005.
239. GEM: A New International Macroeconomic Model, by Tamim Bayoumi, with assistance from Douglas Laxton, Hamid Faruqee, Benjamin Hunt, Philippe Karam, Jaewoo Lee, Alessandro Rebucci, and Ivan Tchakarov. 2004.
238. Stabilization and Reforms in Latin America: A Macroeconomic Perspective on the Experience Since the Early 1990s, by Anoop Singh, Agnès Belaisch, Charles Collyns, Paula De Masi, Reva Krieger, Guy Meredith, and Robert Rennhack. 2005.
237. Sovereign Debt Structure for Crisis Prevention, by Eduardo Borensztein, Marcos Chamon, Olivier Jeanne, Paolo Mauro, and Jeromin Zettelmeyer. 2004.
236. Lessons from the Crisis in Argentina, by Christina Daseking, Atish R. Ghosh, Alun Thomas, and Timothy Lane. 2004.
235. A New Look at Exchange Rate Volatility and Trade Flows, by Peter B. Clark, Natalia Tamirisa, and Shang-Jin Wei, with Azim Sadikov and Li Zeng. 2004.
234. Adopting the Euro in Central Europe: Challenges of the Next Step in European Integration, by Susan M. Schadler, Paulo F. Drummond, Louis Kuijs, Zuzana Murgasova, and Rachel N. van Elkan. 2004.
233. Germany's Three-Pillar Banking System: Cross-Country Perspectives in Europe, by Allan Brunner, Jörg Decressin, Daniel Hardy, and Beata Kudela. 2004.
232. China's Growth and Integration into the World Economy: Prospects and Challenges, edited by Eswar Prasad. 2004.
231. Chile: Policies and Institutions Underpinning Stability and Growth, by Eliot Kalter, Steven Phillips, Marco A. Espinosa-Vega, Rodolfo Luzio, Mauricio Villafuerte, and Manmohan Singh. 2004.
230. Financial Stability in Dollarized Countries, by Anne-Marie Gulde, David Hoelscher, Alain Ize, David Marston, and Gianni De Nicoló. 2004.
229. Evolution and Performance of Exchange Rate Regimes, by Kenneth S. Rogoff, Aasim M. Husain, Ashoka Mody, Robin Brooks, and Nienke Oomes. 2004.
228. Capital Markets and Financial Intermediation in The Baltics, by Alfred Schipke, Christian Beddies, Susan M. George, and Niamh Sheridan. 2004.
227. U.S. Fiscal Policies and Priorities for Long-Run Sustainability, edited by Martin Mühleisen and Christopher Towe 2004.
226. Hong Kong SAR: Meeting the Challenges of Integration with the Mainland, edited by Eswar Prasad, with contributions from Jorge Chan-Lau, Dora Iakova, William Lee, Hong Liang, Ida Liu, Papa N'Diaye, and Tao Wang. 2004.

225. Rules-Based Fiscal Policy in France, Germany, Italy, and Spain, by Teresa Dában, Enrica Detragiache, Gabriel di Bella, Gian Maria Milesi-Ferretti, and Steven Symansky. 2003.

224. Managing Systemic Banking Crises, by a staff team led by David S. Hoelscher and Marc Quintyn. 2003.

223. Monetary Union Among Member Countries of the Gulf Cooperation Council, by a staff team led by Ugo Fasano. 2003.

222. Informal Funds Transfer Systems: An Analysis of the Informal Hawala System, by Mohammed El Qorchi, Samuel Munzele Maimbo, and John F. Wilson. 2003.

221. Deflation: Determinants, Risks, and Policy Options, by Manmohan S. Kumar. 2003.

220. Effects of Financial Globalization on Developing Countries: Some Empirical Evidence, by Eswar S. Prasad, Kenneth Rogoff, Shang-Jin Wei, and Ayhan Kose. 2003.

219. Economic Policy in a Highly Dollarized Economy: The Case of Cambodia, by Mario de Zamaroczy and Sopanha Sa. 2003.

218. Fiscal Vulnerability and Financial Crises in Emerging Market Economies, by Richard Hemming, Michael Kell, and Axel Schimmelpfennig. 2003.

217. Managing Financial Crises: Recent Experience and Lessons for Latin America, edited by Charles Collyns and G. Russell Kincaid. 2003.

216. Is the PRGF Living Up to Expectations?—An Assessment of Program Design, by Sanjeev Gupta, Mark Plant, Benedict Clements, Thomas Dorsey, Emanuele Baldacci, Gabriela Inchauste, Shamsuddin Tareq, and Nita Thacker. 2002.

215. Improving Large Taxpayers' Compliance: A Review of Country Experience, by Katherine Baer. 2002.

214. Advanced Country Experiences with Capital Account Liberalization, by Age Bakker and Bryan Chapple. 2002.

213. The Baltic Countries: Medium-Term Fiscal Issues Related to EU and NATO Accession, by Johannes Mueller, Christian Beddies, Robert Burgess, Vitali Kramarenko, and Joannes Mongardini. 2002.

212. Financial Soundness Indicators: Analytical Aspects and Country Practices, by V. Sundararajan, Charles Enoch, Armida San José, Paul Hilbers, Russell Krueger, Marina Moretti, and Graham Slack. 2002.

211. Capital Account Liberalization and Financial Sector Stability, by a staff team led by Shogo Ishii and Karl Habermeier. 2002.

210. IMF-Supported Programs in Capital Account Crises, by Atish Ghosh, Timothy Lane, Marianne Schulze-Ghattas, Aleš Bulíř, Javier Hamann, and Alex Mourmouras. 2002.

209. Methodology for Current Account and Exchange Rate Assessments, by Peter Isard, Hamid Faruqee, G. Russell Kincaid, and Martin Fetherston. 2001.

208. Yemen in the 1990s: From Unification to Economic Reform, by Klaus Enders, Sherwyn Williams, Nada Choueiri, Yuri Sobolev, and Jan Walliser. 2001.

207. Malaysia: From Crisis to Recovery, by Kanitta Meesook, Il Houng Lee, Olin Liu, Yougesh Khatri, Natalia Tamirisa, Michael Moore, and Mark H. Krysl. 2001.

206. The Dominican Republic: Stabilization, Structural Reform, and Economic Growth, by a staff team led by Philip Young comprising Alessandro Giustiniani, Werner C. Keller, and Randa E. Sab and others. 2001.

205. Stabilization and Savings Funds for Nonrenewable Resources, by Jeffrey Davis, Rolando Ossowski, James Daniel, and Steven Barnett. 2001.

204. Monetary Union in West Africa (ECOWAS): Is It Desirable and How Could It Be Achieved? by Paul Masson and Catherine Pattillo. 2001.

203. Modern Banking and OTC Derivatives Markets: The Transformation of Global Finance and Its Implications for Systemic Risk, by Garry J. Schinasi, R. Sean Craig, Burkhard Drees, and Charles Kramer. 2000.

202. Adopting Inflation Targeting: Practical Issues for Emerging Market Countries, by Andrea Schaechter, Mark R. Stone, and Mark Zelmer. 2000.

Note: For information on the titles and availability of Occasional Papers not listed, please consult the IMF's *Publications Catalog* or contact IMF Publication Services.